Jan Youtz

Dancing with Words

Storytelling as Legacy, Culture, and Faith

D0017830

Ray Buckley

The great Supper
Luke 14:15-24

DISCIPLESHIP RESOURCES

PO BOX 340003 • NASHVILLE, TN 37203-0003
www.discipleshipresources.org

Cover design by Nanci Lamar

Cover Illustration "Shadow Horses" by Carter O. Bock

Cover Beadwork created by unknown Oneida artist, from the collection of JoAnn Catolster Eslinger

Book design by Joey McNair

Edited by Linda R. Whited and David Whitworth

ISBN 0-88177-407-3

Library of Congress Control Number: 2003103585

DR407

Dedication

**To the memory of the
Reverend Dr. Thomas Roughface, Sr.**
Who kept the traditions of the Ponca people, told their stories, and lived his life in service to God and God's people.

**To Dee Brooks, Josephine Buckley, Rick Buckley, Dr.
Barbara Garcia, Dr. Evelyn Laycock, Tom McAnally,
Sharee Johnson, Clancey and Barbara Karst, Gay
Parks, Bishop Sharon Rader, Rev. Wayne and Rev. Jo
Reece, Ginny and John Underwood, Jackie Vaughan,
Della Waghiyi, Dr. Michael Williams, Nancye Willis,
Dayton Edmonds, Freeman Owle, and Bill Wolfe**
Whose lives and stories have challenged and
encouraged mine.

**And to the men, women, and children
of the Oklahoma Indian Missionary Conference**
Who live out the legacy of Native people and serve God
with dedication, love, and joy. Thank you for extending
friendship, fire, and food to one from so far away. You
have been the hand and voice of Christ.

Contents

Author's Note

I have had the gift of knowing people who believed in the value of sharing stories. In the cultures in which I was raised, people told stories easily and joyfully. I have also had the amazing gift of knowing people, among my family and friends, who had confidence in their God and their faith. I owe them a deep debt.

While there are a number of written sources regarding the art of storytelling, storytelling is best learned by listening and then by telling stories. In an attempt to be true to the many roots of storytelling, this resource is a compilation of the experiences of generations of men and women. Much of the information contained in these pages has come from oral traditions surrounding storytelling and storytellers among many cultures. Some information has no written sources. Wherever possible, I have tried to rely on oral traditions. For me, those traditions were first shared by my people, and then came as education from people I have lived among, and from whom I have learned much. In the voices of my Native communities, storytellers in Ghana and Nigeria, Aboriginal storytellers, African American preachers and storytellers, Hispanic teachers, Yaqui and Appalachian storytellers, Inuit and Yupik friends, Native Hawaiian extended family, and my parents and grandparents, has come much of this information. This then is an attempt to place into writing those things which I have learned through the oral/aural transmission of culture and faith.

There is both personal opinion and hypothesis. In attempting to understand the decline and reemergence of storytelling, I have put forth some personal thoughts and beliefs related to historical events.

In all, this is a gathering of experience from many people who have taught me over the years. I share it with you, as it has been shared with me: freely, fearfully, joyfully, and with love.

Ray Buckley
Palmer, Alaska

Introduction
Why Storytelling?

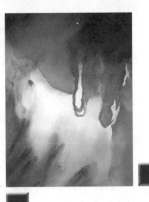

*I*t was her shoes that I always noticed first. They seemed much too large and heavy for such a small person. Still, they had carried her feet for many miles and must have seemed like old, trusted friends. They bore the scars of rocks and brush and the occasional pavement that had attempted to thwart their determined destiny.

From where I sat on the ground, I could see that her brown stockings fell into friendly wrinkles that seemed to match those on her hands and arms and cheeks. It was as if everything about her was in agreement and assumed a comfortable position. Far below her knees, the hem of a cotton dress met the stockings. Careful washing had dulled its color, and it gracefully carried the even lighter shade of where her hands had rested on her knees over many years. Around and above her waist was a collection of rounded, gentle shapes that included several cotton bags filled with extraordinary surprises and a light shawl that served as cover and a portable throne.

She was always slightly bent, but when she leaned over a child, one could see all of her journeys traced on her face. They ran softly around the chin and enveloped the ears. They meandered around her cheeks, leaving two smooth places. They found a home around her eyes and played there awhile before moving gently into the wisps of white hair that became a stream of braid down her back.

There was an enormous comfort to her. I loved the "coming-toward-me" side of her because it filled me with joy. There was a welcoming to her that seemed like a perpetual invitation. I do not choose to remember the "going-away" side as well because there was an empty spot in any place when she was no longer there.

She was named well. She was named after the black-tailed deer that lived in the grasslands. When she was young, her light form and large eyes must have brought to mind those small, delicate deer that hid in cottonwood tree groves. We called her "Grandma," not only because we called most elderly women "Grandma" but also because she knew us all by name and could tell us the names of our ancestors and the adventures they had known. She knew the sacred stories and the comic ones. She knew stories of brave men and even braver women. She knew stories of the animals and Those That Crawled. She knew the stories of the First Beginnings. She kept stories like she kept the treasures in her bags. She wore them as comfortably as the shawl and stockings. Some seemed enormous and weighty, like her shoes.

There was a protocol to our listening. If we began talking, she would simply stop and walk away. The story may not have continued until days later. Some stories were selectively shared, waiting for the right moment or audience. They were, after all, a gift to be opened and delighted in, and gifts were chosen carefully. She watched our faces as the story-gifts were revealed, taking delight in our delight. We listened with ears and eyes, merging sight and sound into an almost tangible form. We listened for key words, which were emphasized by slowing the language, leaning forward, and asking with the eyes, "Did you hear it? Did you catch the importance?"

Her voice was soft. One had to listen intently. Seldom was it raised. Sometimes the words came quickly, sometimes slowly. There were moments when the story was moving at you. Sometimes she would pause and breathe in deeply, as if she were pulling you into the place where the story began. The sharing of the story was not without the sharing of self. The story had become part of the shoes and the brown stockings. It had become part of the soft wrinkles and the white braid.

From the first words, "This is my story . . . ," we were drawn into the tale, as if those words were a cue for our brains to shift from the present reality into a place where we were feeling, smelling, and tasting the world of the story. Her eyes, voice, smile, hands, and posture conveyed countless pieces of nonverbal information. She chose her words carefully, like one would choose marbles from a glass jar. Silence itself was a chosen word-turned-paragraph. A gesture, frozen in midair, became an exclamation point. She was a dancer whose legs no longer moved well. She painted with colors we saw in our minds. She was a weaver of words, handing one a basket woven of thought. But when it was complete the basket became ours.

I have a collection of these baskets in my memory. They are part of my mind and spirit. They have become woven into my psyche. They were the gift of the storyteller as we wove them together—her stories and our imaginations. The concepts have broadened as I have become older. Many of the characters have become metaphors. Many of the words have developed into ideas. The morals have influenced my behavior. The values have become part of who I am.

We became a community, those of us who listened. We were united by story. We were united by imagery. We had a moment of combined history and imagination. The words bound us to our cultures. The experiences of the characters became our experiences brought to life by the storyteller. She "breathed to life" the story and in doing so breathed the same life into a part of us.

Growing up, I would listen to our Lakota elders speaking of their life experiences. In the stories they told and in the way they greeted each other were three beautiful words heard over and over. In her beautiful book *Bead on an Anthill: A Lakota Childhood* (University of Nebraska Press, 1998), Delphine Red Shirt placed them together. Seeing those words together, almost like a poem, has placed them indelibly in my memory. I never think of them apart from one another.

> *Weksuye* (Wek [*e* as in they]-soo-yeh)—I remember
> *Ciksuye* (Cik [*c* as in chair, *i* as in mill]-soo-yeh)—I remember you
> *Miksuye* (Mik [*i* as in mill]-soo-yeh)—Remember me

Somewhere in the process of storytelling, the story becomes memory. If the story has connected with our spirits, then that memory is the gift of the storyteller. We are able to say: I remember. This is a part of me. These are things of importance to me. This collective experience of storytelling has been internalized into collective memory. The visual images are ones we share. *Weksuye. I remember.*

I remember you. I remember how you moved and spoke. I remember the things you did, the words you chose, and how you believed. I remember the essence of who you were. I remember you, though we were generations apart. You have become part of my active memory and have impacted the things that I celebrate, enjoy, and believe. I remember you, because others remembered you and kept you alive. *Ciksuye. I remember you.*

Remember me. I tell you of the things I feel and have experienced. They are part of who I am. When the living reminders of my life have passed on, these are the songs, words, events, prayers, actions, joys, sorrows, triumphs, defeats, dances, and solitary moments that have been a part of me. These things have become part of the story. If they have value for you, in whatever time and place you find yourself—remember me. *Miksuye. Remember me!*

We choose to remember for the purpose of sharing stories. Storytelling affirms for us the memory of our people, whoever they may be. Long before the written word or the printing press, those who first told and remembered the stories passed on a legacy as human beings. We are people of the story, and we seek to identify and tell our stories in nearly everything we do.

Storytelling has significance in child development. A child responds to the rhythm of the language of nursery rhymes by moving her arms and legs. A child responds to the animated face and voice of a parent with the animation of his own face and voice. Storytelling becomes a vehicle by which children develop communication tools and listening skills. In *The Arts and Human Development* (John Wiley & Sons, 1973; page 203), Howard Gardner reminds us that storytelling fully captures a child's attention. Characters become important to a child, and they will be incorporated into the way the child experiences events during the day. Children will also use characters in story as role-play models. Children respond to story in an almost mystical way.

A child relates storytelling (the telling of a story) to human contact, and that contact becomes as much a part of the story as the story itself. As adults, we experience storytelling in much the same fashion. Isn't it interesting that in many cultures, storytelling is viewed as a form of touch?

Modern studies indicate that the adult human body begins to relax when listening to a story, in ways not associated with other mediums. Almost as soon as a story is begun, the mind seems to shift from our multitasking operations into a listening and experiencing that involves both the mind and the body. The responses that we learned in childhood begin almost as soon as the first words are spoken, and our minds identify the event as the sharing of a story.

The face-to-face communication that exists between a storyteller and those listening elicits a different response in the body. Several studies indicate that when we encounter another human being face-to-face, the majority of the information transmitted is nonverbal. Simply put, there is a difference in how we respond as human beings to another physically present person sharing information. Much of that response is due not so much to the words of the story as to the reaction of the storyteller to the story itself and his or her conscious, and unconscious, ways of telling the story.

Storytelling at its best is an interaction between storyteller and story-listener. The vehicle is the story, but the experience can be as engaging as an intimate conversation. The human mind and thus the body respond to storytelling as a signal of closeness and intimacy. Story itself couches history, values, culture, faith, life lessons, and other critical elements in a manner easily assimilated in memory. Story shared with conviction and appreciation creates an emotional link.

As people of faith, storytelling has special meaning for us. If all revelation is relationship, then storytelling becomes testimony, or the sharing of another's testimony, to relationship. The act of storytelling itself becomes relational. It extends beyond the bounds of *instructive* or *entertaining* to become *connectional.* The storyteller engages the listener relationally. The listener responds to the story and the storyteller. The listener seeks credibility in the voice, posture, and nonverbal communication of the storyteller. The storyteller responds to the face of the listener. We are people of The Story.

We are able to testify. We are able to say, *I remember. I remember you. Remember me.* And we tell The Story.

The Psalmist penned so eloquently:

> Give ear, O my people, to my teaching;
>   incline your ears to the words of my mouth.
> I will open my mouth in a parable;
>   I will utter dark sayings from of old,
> things that we have heard and known,
>   that our ancestors have told us.
> We will not hide them from their children;
>   we will tell to the coming generation
> the glorious deeds of the LORD, and his might,
>   and the wonders that he has done.
>
>   Psalm 78:1-4

Come, and sit awhile. Listen to the things I want to tell you. Listen with your whole being. I want to tell you a story. A story that began in times we can no longer see clearly. It is a story of things that we have heard and known for ourselves. It is a story that our ancestors began. We must tell the story so that the children of their children's children will know it. We will tell our children of all the things that God has done, both glorious and mighty.

We are people of The Story.

Part I
The Legacy of Storytelling

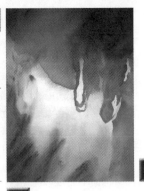

The Heritage

*A*mong many Native American cultures, and those of other indigenous peoples, the meaning of the word used to describe themselves or given to themselves as a name is often "human-being" or "real people." It is important for us to identify ourselves within a community and to recognize ourselves as "people" or part of "a people." At its essence, storytelling is sheer celebration of the fact that we are not alone.

Human beings have a basic need for community. Our family groups are permanent, linked by bonds across great distances. At the base of who we are is the need to find others who are like us or, if not like us, enough like us to live in cohabitation. We mistrust those human beings who seem to not need the approval of our community. We seek each other out.

One of the ways in which we have found community is the sharing of story. Sometimes it is the sharing of a specific story or a common experience of survival that has bound us together. We repeat those stories as a way to cement social bonds and to share with other people and generations those community-binding experiences. We have preserved those stories that have significant meaning to us, and by that selective preservation we tell others about our values. We create stories that reflect our values, thereby preserving those values through our new stories.

All stories have a beginning. All societies have a place of beginning and an event that marks their emergence as a culture. Emergence stories play a significant role in every culture. They are not necessarily creation stories, but they are stories that mark the point where a culture identifies its beginning as a unique people. Many emergence stories contain elements of the cosmology, or worldview, of their culture. Many have their origin in crisis. Something happened that made us "a people."

Oral Tradition

Through the use of oral tradition, or storytelling, communities have maintained their identities by preserving for their children, and their children's children, the unique aspects of their cultures, including religion, ethics, values, art, science, and history. Sometimes values and culture have been carefully integrated and woven into story form as a vehicle of communication. Other oral histories are simply that, a carefully preserved genealogy and legacy of a people transmitted and preserved by each generation. What remains is what generation after generation has maintained as being essential to define themselves.

All historical cultures have oral traditions. Until people groups acquired written language through cultural development or contact with other cultures, storytellers acted as the preservers of culture. While the ability to read was a luxury reserved for those with the opportunity for formal education, storytellers remained the primary vehicle for cultural transmission and preservation. Many of the first forms of literature were the recordings of oral traditions dating back thousands of years.

Oral traditions can be remarkably accurate to the smallest detail. The Supreme Court of Canada recognizes the oral histories of its Aboriginal or First Nations Peoples as admissible evidence in court.

Language

Language is a critical element in storytelling. The languages in which stories were and are created cradle and infuse those stories. The language of a people, like its stories, reflects the values of a people. Societies create and preserve words that express meaning for that society. Native Hawaiians, for instance, have many words for waves. Each term may describe the mood, intensity, shape, and impact on human beings of waves. But we understand, if we know the language, the importance of choosing a specific word, which may describe for us what is happening behind the wave and how it may impact us. The cultural significance of a word like *wave* may be lost without the language of the storyteller.

Language is still vitally critical to culture and storytelling. Many cultures, faced with new terminology such as *car, telephone,* or *computer,* have created new compound words using traditional concepts rather than compromise their language. My grandfather could not afford a telephone until later in life. When he acquired one, he used the phrase "It cries a lot" to refer to it. This described not only the sound of the telephone but its intrusion, which was a cultural anathema. Among some Chukchi (one of the Native people groups of Siberia) the computer is known as "box-of-Other-things." *Other* is a proper noun referring to that which is outside of Chukchi social protocol, where information is shared face-to-face.

Stories Preserve Culture and Values

Stories are tools used to communicate with and, perhaps, communalize those who are listening. But in a real sense, a story assumes a life. Because stories preserve culture and values, retelling stories to new audiences and new generations has the potential to inspire action or change. It is the motivating or delighting aspects of stories that seem to give them a life of their own.

Because of the potential of encouraging a specific human response, many cultures view their stories as entities. My ancestors believed that stories were living, breathing beings brought into life by the telling. As unusual as that might seem for us, there is a strong reality to that belief. Stories have the potential to "bring to life" individuals, values, history, and faith. Some stories can produce strong emotional response. It is also that same potential for response in a story that carefully guards the protocol surrounding its use. Traditional stories may have strict taboos regarding their use and application. Respecting the potential of a story is giving honor to the story itself as well as those who listen.

Gender and Storytelling

As we examine the history and importance of storytelling, a key element is the role of gender. Why gender? In most cultures of the world, the first story a child hears is through its mother. There may be the added voices of grandmothers, aunts, older female siblings, and extended family. Although male members of any culture also play a strong role in transmitting culture, their roles are generally more specific. It is women who most often develop the sense of comfort a child feels when listening to a story. From women, in most cultures, the child learns to associate physical touch and story, as well as a sense of well-being. Women have been the primary culture bearers of every society, and women are almost always the initial educators of children.

While the world is quickly moving toward a westernized society, it is important to understand that the vast majority of cultures in the world are not European or North American. What we have come to view as the popular culture of the world is not the culture from which most of the world emerges. While Western civilization for hundreds of years denigrated the status of women, that is not always the experience of other cultures. Stories from around the world are written from the perspective of women as primary characters. Heroes may be women. Only women tell some stories. Only men tell others.

Many indigenous cultures are matriarchal, tracing their lineage not through their fathers, but through their mothers. Some languages, such as Lakota, have a female and a male voice. Many cultures believed that the ability to conceive and carry a child is the greatest power a human can possess. Among some Native cultures, adult women were forbidden to tell some stories, not because of gender in the strictest sense, but because the power of being able to conceive was more powerful than the story itself. Many women became strong spiritual leaders, most often after menopause. Spiritual leaders, in most indigenous communities, were culture bearers and storytellers.

The ability to have children meant that *a people* would survive. The ability to transfer the language, culture, and values to children meant that *a culture* would survive. While cultural specifics may be passed along during a lifetime, language and cultural identity are passed along between birth and four years. Women carried the weight of language and cultural priorities.

To our women of many cultures we owe the preservation of many of the world's stories.

Storytelling Across Cultures

Native Traditions

Among Native people in much of North America, while storytelling is often entertaining, most stories contain significant cultural and religious information. Some tribes restricted storytelling to certain times of the year, often when food had been harvested and prepared for the long winter. Some stories accompanied specific religious and social events. Oral histories were transmitted from generation to generation. Children who had strong memories were identified and taught early the traditions of their people. If asked to tell a story, a person would often defer to the oldest elder still telling that particular story. When it was appropriate, stories, like songs, were "gifted" to another, who then carried the responsibility of the story.

Honesty and humility are highly valued. Among Northern Plains tribes, a warrior returning from battle or a successful hunt would be expected to recount his victory in the form of a story. This storytelling was not bragging but an accounting to the community of his actions. Another warrior was required to verify the actions. From that point on, most warriors no longer spoke of their victories. Native people from most traditions do not speak of their successes. Someone in the community will speak for them when necessary. Humility is maintained, as well as accountability.

In Native communities, individuals were valued for their gifts to the people. There are many documented accounts of people with disabilities who were exceptional spiritual leaders, storytellers, and artisans.

Some cultures combined storytelling and dance, with elaborate tales being acted out over an evening or days. Many forms of dancing and storytelling are also prayers, and they are not performed for those outside of the community.

During the early Reservation Period, oral traditions still remained strong. Because federal law prohibited the practice of many Native traditions, some were carried out in secret. Native children were forcibly removed from their homes at an early age and sent to boarding schools where they were forbidden to speak their tribal languages or practice their cultures. They were taught to read by reading the Bible, and the same people who taught them to read the Bible beat them if they spoke their languages. For the protection of their children, many elders did not teach them tribal languages, and refused to pass on their stories or oral traditions. But there were many who tenaciously preserved their cultures. One-half of tribal languages still remain.

African Traditions

Thousands of years before Europe was engaged in the Crusades, great tribal cultures flourished in Africa. Across that vast and diverse continent, cultures existed with remarkable trade, economics, music, science, medicine, literature, philosophy, religion—and storytelling. Storytellers in many parts of Africa were paid, if the audience appreciated the story. Storytelling was often interactive. Portions of the story would call for the audience to sing, dance, or act out. People in the audience could argue with characters. Listeners, who would respond out loud, could affirm characters or comments within the story. The "call and response" familiar in African American churches today descends from African traditions of storytelling.

The slave trade, which tore apart families and communities and forced millions of souls from their homes, had an unusual consequence. The cultures of Africa were taken around the world. The skills, music, philosophy, and voices of Africa were carried to portions of Europe and the Middle East, and across the Atlantic to North and South America.

It is my conclusion that all we know as the existing cultures of the Americas and the Caribbean, and extending far beyond, would not exist without the skills and cultures of those who came against their will from Africa and their descendants. Storytelling and story-songs were among the many traditions that knitted African-descended communities together. African American communities have cultural similarities, but there are also regional distinctions that add to the broad cultural base of American society. As we will see, some of the revival and preservation of storytelling as an art form, and certainly as a worship tool, is fundamentally linked to communities of African heritage.

Aboriginal Traditions

One of the cultures with the strongest tradition of storytelling is that of the Aboriginal people of Australia. Storytellers were often born into the role, with stories passed down by female members of a given community. Like Native stories, Aboriginal stories existed in categories dictated by protocols within a given community. There were stories that could be told publicly, sacred stories shared with the community, and sacred stories that were secret in nature. There were stories that only women could tell, and stories that only men could tell.

Aboriginal stories of creation are known as *Dreamtime stories.* Such stories may be complex, with multiple layers of spiritual beliefs and values. Each story may contain many lessons, and each region may have different stories or interpretations of stories. There are more than seven hundred variations on the Aboriginal language base, so stories often have key ingredients that relate to a specific community.

Folktales

Folktales from around the world include such interesting devices as riddles, the guessing of names as a reversal of magic, or songs sung in pieces throughout the story yet constituting a whole. The use of secret names by folklore characters appears often in stories from all over the world. Folktales include fairy tales, epic tales, and stories involving magic and magical creatures. Most cultures of the world include stories of "little people."

Jewish Traditions

In many countries around the world, Jewish communities were storytelling greenhouses. Storytelling was an essential component of community and religious life. Stories contained in Jewish literature were also part of oral tradition. Many of the world's best-known stories are part of the cultural and religious traditions of Hasidic communities. Hasidic tradition includes the use of storytelling in the introduction of belief systems and rituals to children. Perhaps more than any culture, Jewish communities preserved both the oral and written stories, resulting in a rich heritage of stories appreciated the world over.

Following the devastating persecution in Russia and the Holocaust of World War II, many communities were broken up. Survivors came together in other parts of the world, bringing with them both oral and literary traditions.

Hispanic Traditions

There are many distinct cultures in the group of people we call Hispanic. Oral traditions are as varied as the cultures from which they arise. Native, Spanish, and African influences are all seen in stories from Hispanic peoples. From Cuba, Puerto Rico, the Caribbean, Mexico, and Central and South America, as well as large portions of the United States, Hispanic culture developed regionally with unique storytelling traditions. Hispanic oral traditions also include a variety of religious influences as well. To protect Native stories, some are couched in forms acceptable to the church. Like African American stories, Hispanic stories often contain elements far older than European settlement. Both men and women share stories.

In Hispanic communities, the tradition of storytelling remained intact, and the movement of people of Hispanic heritage throughout the Western Hemisphere helped facilitate the revival of the storytelling art form.

The Appalachian-Mountains Traditions

In the American southeast, Scottish and Irish immigrants fleeing political conflicts settled in the safety of the Appalachian Mountains. The geography of these mountain regions provided relative isolation and a cultural cloister in which music, crafts, religion, philosophy, and storytelling developed in unique forms. While poverty led many mountain people to urban centers, mountain culture remained as solid as the people who gave it birth.

Other Traditions

Even as people left traditional communities for jobs in big cities, unique cultural pockets still remained. German settlers in Texas, Norwegian and Swedish farmers in the Midwest, Cajun communities in Louisiana, and hundreds more found strength in common culture.

The Decline of Storytelling

One of the first rules of storytelling is to avoid lengthy passages of information. Another would be to avoid the Dark and Middle Ages in Europe. Unfortunately, you're not in luck! Since in many indigenous and ethnic communities storytelling remained a vital form of society, when we look at the decline of storytelling, we are looking largely at the influences which altered European history and spread to North America.

During the Middle Ages in Europe, only the wealthy could afford education. The ability to read and write was limited to nobility and church clerics. In the feudal structure of European states, the peasant class existed to serve the wealthy landowners, and the poor were expendable. Cathedrals were built not only to honor God but also to awe the poor into accepting the power of both the state and the church as the will of God. Stained-glass windows became the illustrations of Bible stories, and the poor studied the images to recall Bible stories.

Knights returning from the Crusades brought with them tales of war and adventure, as well as cultural traditions and stories from the Middle East. Storytellers were a vital part of community life. Affluent and influential, professional storytellers preserved both history and culture, and like Middle Eastern storytellers, they served to distribute information. The terms *bard* and *troubadour* are often associated with the traveling storytellers of the Middle Ages.

While the peasant class did not have access to the arts and education in a formal sense, communities continued traditions that reached to their roots: folk arts. Folk medicine, music, dance, art, and storytelling remained as integral parts of community life. In every village individuals were recognized and valued for their unique talents and skills. In these communities, storytelling flourished, and several hundred years later, the descendants of these communities would play a role in bringing storytelling back.

During the Renaissance period, all of the arts flourished to grand levels. Storytellers were found in every court. At the same time, classical drama, inherited from the Greeks and once banned by the church, was taking on new forms and reemerging throughout Europe.

While many historians associate the invention of the printing press (Gutenberg press) as a primary cause in the decline of the influence of storytellers, there may be other factors that had greater impact. While the printing press enabled books to be printed instead of being hand-scribed, the majority of the population still could not read, let alone afford a book. It would be several hundred years before most of the population had affordable access to books. What began to change in new directions was how we began to view each other.

Individual Worth Versus Productivity

A remarkable change took place as agrarian cultures became industrialized, both in Europe and in the New World. Villages remained essentially the same. But urban centers attracted the poor, and new industries depended on a work force. Seasonal work was replaced by new concepts of productivity. Men, women, and children worked six days a week, sometimes sixteen hours a day.

It would seem to me that one of the results of industrialization, from a human standpoint, was a dramatic shift in perspective and value regarding human worth. Access to the arts became increasingly a preoccupation of the wealthy. In an industrialized world, individual worth was measured in what a person was able to produce, not in his or her intrinsic value to the community, and there were always people needing work. There was little time for stories, and oral tradition had no place in a society that no longer valued those traditions. Storytelling was often viewed as an activity for children. Adults did not go to listen to storytellers, and storytellers themselves had few opportunities to share their stories. For a while it seemed that storytelling was a forgotten art.

By the ending of World War I, more people worldwide were moving to industrialized cities, and cultural communities were struggling to survive.

There were other changes at the end of World War II. The war itself had brought an exchange of cultures. People from many countries tended to see themselves less as cultural entities and began to see themselves through nationalistic eyes. As the world turned from a war economy to rebuilding, radio and eventually television made the world even smaller. Increasingly, jobs were available only in the city. Values changed. Time was measured not by the seasons but by the time clock. We were beginning the move from industrialization into the age of technology.

As technology became affordable and society became production oriented, stories were told through different mediums. Most adults considered storytellers to be those who read to children. One could listen to or watch stories and not be a participant.

One could listen to a story and be alone.

Storytelling Reemerges

We are all familiar with the phrase "alone in a crowd." Many people describe the sensation of being surrounded by people yet feeling alone. For whatever reason, without human interaction, human contact may be as isolating as being stranded on a desert island. Many people attend church services every Sunday without meaningful interaction. People ride subways in urban centers without speaking to one another. Many of us lack the ability to even determine our own supply of basic needs. We cannot grow our own food. We cannot supply our own warmth. The vast majority of the people in the world will never own or build their own homes. We are perhaps the most technologically advanced and informed society in the history of the world, yet we are also the most dependent on technology and most disconnected from each other.

Across the world, more and more people are becoming collectors. Do you know what category of collectibles is sought after the most? We call it nostalgia. They are the things from our childhoods, or our parents' childhoods, things that give us feelings of comfort and deep meaning. Have you ever visited a friend's home where nostalgic items are displayed? What happens? A story. People observe an article of clothing, a lunchbox, a tool, and begin to tell stories of their meaning. We have found something in common, something to share, a way to reveal something about ourselves that says, "This has meaning for me."

Storytelling reemerged because in the middle of our busy lives human-to-human contact was absent. We needed to say, "This is me." Our children no longer knew from where they had come. We passed each other on the freeway every day and never knew what there was to celebrate about each other. Storytelling reemerged when we discovered what we had already known, that when we talked together, when we got to know each other, there was much in common.

Civil Rights and Cultural Awareness

One factor in North America that we seldom consider in the revival of folk arts, including storytelling, is the Civil Rights Movement of the 1960's. People of African descent began to explore their rich heritage from Africa, including music, art, dance, textiles, and storytelling. In addition, we began to examine the cultures of slave communities and the divergent cultures of African American communities after the abolishment of the institution of slavery. We began to think of the growing, vital, developing African American cultures.

The Civil Rights Movement, which began as a movement for equal rights among African American communities, had profound effects in other communities as well. Native American communities were beginning to feel a revitalization of traditional cultures, including art, religion, traditional values, ... and storytelling. With the push for civil rights among migrant workers in California and the southwest, young Hispanics began exploring traditions, customs, and art forms. Apart from civil rights issues, a side effect of these movements was a rediscovery of uniqueness and a renewed sense of community.

The cultural awareness that followed the civil rights movement also impacted other communities. For many years the mountain people of Virginia, West Virginia, Kentucky, Tennessee, and North Carolina had slowly been migrating into the urban centers of the East to find employment in industry. Many had brought the folk arts and the values of the mountains with them, but there had not always been an appreciation of the unique expressions of the Appalachians. During the late 1960's and the 1970's we began to see a resurgence and valuing of the mountain cultures, including the rich tradition of storytelling.

Across the United States and into Europe there was a growing appreciation of the uniqueness of communities. We talked more about Amish and Hutterite communities, the distinctiveness of New Mexican Hispanic art forms, Celtic music and stories, Norwegian/Swedish/German traditions of the Midwest, Welsh singing, Southern folk traditions and storytelling, Bluegrass, the music of Newfoundland and Nova Scotia, Bonsai, Karate, Thai cuisine, Cowboy stories, and poetry. We found value in the uniqueness of each other, and we began to have a desire to experience each other. We were looking backward into our cultures as a way to find comfort and family. We needed to feel we were not alone.

Public Libraries

We owe a great deal to public libraries. Public libraries were venues for storytellers. Sometimes people would read a book, but increasingly they would *tell* stories. Libraries became resources for experienced storytellers and also venues for those trying their wings.

Storytellers would come together and simply tell stories as a means of developing community. In doing so, they would share ideas. To storytelling events would be added workshops and resources. Around the world, storytelling festivals sprang up. Events were no longer just for storytellers but were for those who wanted to come and listen to stories as well. The art form that had suffered due to industrialization, changing values, and technology had come full circle.

We were coming home.

Stories and Faith

It is the same phrase in every translation of the Bible. In Hebrew, English, Swahili, Mayan, and Chukchi, the words are the same. "In the beginning, God ..."

"In the beginning ..." This is the place where the story begins. Well, actually, not really, but that is part of the story line yet to be realized. "In the beginning," though, is where the storyteller chooses to begin the story. Dry land emerges. Light comes into the world and everything is changed. Plants and trees grow, fish swim, and birds fly. God creates man and woman, and the purpose of the story is revealed. *We are never alone.*

Oral traditions in regard to Scripture or sacred text are those stories that existed primarily through oral transmission and contributed to or helped compose a text written later. The Pentateuch (Genesis, Exodus, Leviticus, Numbers, and Deuteronomy) is generally attributed to Moses. Scholars estimate that many of the stories included in the book of Genesis predate the life of Moses by nearly a thousand years. Passed down through generations, the stories of the creation and fall, Enoch, Noah and the flood, Abraham and Sarah, Isaac and Rebekah, Jacob and Rachel, and Joseph were part of an oral tradition, which also survived four hundred years of slavery in Egypt. Memories of places and events were preserved as story because they were significant to culture and faith.

The Book of Job, considered one of the greatest pieces of literature of all time, most certainly existed in part as oral tradition before being written. Indeed, much of what we consider pre-Christian sacred writings (Old Testament, Septuagint, and so forth) existed in part as oral tradition. Literature additionally became source material for storytelling in both organized and itinerant venues.

Jewish oral traditions remind us of the role of storytelling in Hebrew society. In Judaic culture, members of the tribe of Levi, from which came the priests, were known for their storytelling abilities. The people of greatest influence in any culture are those who teach young children. Hebrew women, who provided early education at home, were gifted storytellers who used storytelling as a teaching tool.

Among biblical cultures, telling a story was a high art form, and both kings and people in public markets cherished storytellers. Storytellers were paid for their work. A good storyteller was not only entertaining but also served to convey news. Traveling often, storytellers passed information from community to community. Storytellers often accompanied armies, not only to record events but also to develop oral accounts and songs about victories to be used in homecoming celebrations. Stories carried home from other cultures served to transmit new philosophies and ideas.

Jesus

Jesus was a storyteller. When crowds gathered around him, Jesus often told them stories to illustrate spiritual truths. The Synoptic Gospels record no fewer than forty parables in the messages of Jesus.

Through simple, clear stories, Jesus spoke to the crowds who followed him in a manner that was familiar to their culture, but not necessarily the way of one educated in the Law. The message of Jesus was one of relationship, and he chose a relational way to share that message. The disciples and the apostles would share those same stories. Those stories would be carried throughout the known world. They would be told and retold. When the writers of the Synoptic Gospels, through the inspiration of the Holy Spirit, penned their books, they drew on common sources, interviews, and oral traditions. John Mark drew heavily on the stories and sermons of Peter pertaining to the life of Christ. It is a common belief that today the parables of Jesus are the most quoted passages of the Bible, next to the Twenty-third Psalm and John 3:16.

The Parable of the Prodigal and His Brother

There was a man who had two sons. The younger of them said to his father, "Father, give me the share of the property that will belong to me." So [the father] divided his property between them. A few days later the younger son gathered all he had and traveled to a distant country, and there he squandered his property in dissolute living. When he had spent everything, a severe famine took place throughout that country, and he began to be in need. So he went and hired himself out to one of the citizens of that country, who sent him to his fields to feed the pigs. He would gladly have filled himself with the pods that the pigs were eating; and no one gave him anything. But when he came to himself he said, "How many of my father's hired hands have bread enough and to spare, but here I am dying of hunger! I will get up and go to my father, and I will say to him, 'Father, I have sinned against heaven and before you; I am no longer worthy to be called your son; treat me like one of your hired hands.'" So he set off and went to his father. But while he was still far off, his father saw him and was filled with compassion; he ran and put his arms around him and kissed him. Then the son said to him, "Father, I have sinned against heaven and before you; I am no longer worthy to be called your son." But the father said to his slaves, "Quickly, bring out a robe—the best one—and put it on him; put a ring on his finger and sandals on his feet. And get the fatted calf and kill it, and let us eat and celebrate; for this son of mine was dead and is alive again; he was lost and is found!" And they began to celebrate.

Now his elder son was in the field; and when he came and approached the house, he heard music and dancing. He called one of the slaves and asked what was going on. [The slave] replied, "Your brother has come, and your father has killed the fatted calf, because he has got him back safe and sound." Then [the elder son] became angry and refused to go in. His father came out and began to plead with him. But he answered his father, "Listen! For all these years I have been working like a slave for you, and I have never disobeyed your command; yet you have never given me even a young goat so that I might celebrate with my friends. But when this son of yours came back, who has devoured your property with prostitutes, you killed the fatted calf for him!" Then the father said to him, "Son, you are always with me, and all that is mine is yours. But we had to celebrate and rejoice, because this brother of yours was dead and has come to life; he was lost and has been found."

(Luke 15:11-32)

As we will see later, in this one story alone are all of the elements of a good story. There is primarily an intent in language and style to speak in ways that would allow those listening to understand and also remember. Jesus was not speaking *at* the crowd; he was interacting *with* the crowd. Jesus anticipated the needs of the people. He fed them and taught them using stories. By the style and language he chose, Jesus was also clearly defining his theology: God wants to interact with us. You are not alone.

The birth, life, ministry, death, and resurrection of Jesus would come to be known as The Story.

It is clear from the Acts of the Apostles (the companion volume to Luke) that the early evangelists and missionaries of the Christian community continued to use Jesus' method of storytelling as a primary means of sharing the gospel. Paul's eloquent testimony before Agrippa is an example of oral tradition surrounding the life of Jesus as well as a description of Paul's encounter with the living Christ on the road to Damascus. Testimony is one of the purest forms of storytelling, and one of the most compelling.

Stories and Healing

Our life events become "our stories," and those who know us, or know about us, pass them along for various reasons. Fame, it might be said, is society's recognition and fascination with our "story," whether momentary or heroic. And medical science recognizes that there is both physical and psychological healing associated with the telling of our personal stories. As we are able to share our stories and find validation among our communities, we seem to be able to affirm and identify the positives in our stories and confront the conflicts. In the same sense, *others* who hear *our* stories and relate to our experiences cease to be *others* and are pulled into community *with us*. It is in the act of sharing our stories that all are made aware that "I am not alone."

So too, stories become vehicles of healing. In many cultures, certain stories (or story-songs) were recognized for contributing to a healing response in people. Some stories helped restore a sense of community. Some stories helped restore a sense of newness. Others, as part of an extensive ritual, served to assist in a rite of passage. Our ancestors recognized that some stories brought about physiological changes, and by couching concepts in story, they drew forth a physiological response different from what arose from merely sharing ideas. Some stories share joy. Other stories share awareness. Many offer hope.

Several years ago, when non-Hodgkin's lymphoma became a name that I would wear for many months, I sat in a room with other cancer patients. Most of us were in various stages of baldness, but I felt particularly naked, having lost a mustache, beard, and all of my hair. I've never been a small person, but several months of steroids had made me resemble a steer getting ready for the state fair. I had found a Harley-Davidson bandana, which offered some pretension of toughness, and had bought one for my dog, who, having all of her hair, saw no need to like it at all.

Across the room, two small girls wearing scarves were giggling and peeking around their parents, who were obviously mortified. During the time we drank a Kool-Aidy drink and had the last of the cookies from the week before, a small hand pulled on my sweater. I looked down into two large green eyes, freckles, and a smile that would have been sparkling if it had had all of its teeth. Putting a hand over the jack-o-lantern smile, the little face said matter-of-factly, "You look just like Uncle Fester." Visions of the Addams Family character came into my mind. Bald head, with a glowing light bulb in his mouth. In my turtleneck sweater, bald head, lip, chin, and state-fair deportment, I was a poster ready to be hung. The little face nodded. The jack-o-lantern lips got bigger and turned upward.

It was at a garage sale two weeks later that I found them. Not one, but two remnants of a light bulb salesman's giveaways. "Magical" light bulbs that, when touched, lit up. The dog and my brother stood with wide eyes as I tested to make sure I wouldn't die from shock. I imagined myself being electrocuted and having no hair to stand up.

I touched the end of one bulb with my finger. It lit. I touched my finger to my tongue and then touched the bulb. It lit. Carefully, I placed the end of the bulb in my mouth. I did not die. I stood, baldheaded with light bulb glowing.

I waited for my chance. I waited until the room was still, and all of us bald folks were quiet. I found her sitting across the room. For a moment I caught her eye, and then slowly, I did the miraculous. From my pocket I took out the light bulb and placed it into my mouth, and lit up the room!

We were on odd pair. Uncle Fester and a little jack-o-lantern, each lit up and glowing, looking out into the snow like two Christmas bulbs.

Often, storytellers were viewed as healers. Or healers, in some communities, were also storytellers. For our ancestors and for many cultures today those who share the gift of story have a role in healing and restoring a sense of community. Modern medical and psychological sciences recognize the role of familiar ritual within a community setting as a powerful tool for breaking through the isolation of illness in all of its forms. Storytelling for the critically ill or those with mental illness is a gift that brings warmth and restores a sense of community and familiarity.

It was late in October, and the leaves were already off of the trees. A few hung on to remind us of their existence and quietly waved at us as we passed by. The grasses had grown tall with their last autumnal burst, glad for the cooler weather and rain.

Dad was driving our '57 Chevy, which was new to us, although it was a decade old. We carefully washed its whitewalls, so that they would shine in the sunlight, but that day our tires sunk up to the hubcaps in the muddy road.

Around the soggy road were grasses and trees. We had left the few houses miles back. Dad seemed to recognize one tree and we stopped the car in the road, reasonably assured that there would be no others along that way. To the left was a long driveway, really just two tire-tracks through the grass. At the end, barely visible, was an old house with a small porch, on which clung a few dried flecks of paint. We stepped into the mud and walked toward the house.

No one knew we were coming (Dad said they had no electricity), but an old-looking young woman stood on the porch. She nodded at us, and said quietly, "He thought you might come." Two pairs of muddy shoes, one big and one small, were left on the porch.

There was a bedroom in this house. In the bed, covered with a star-quilt, a man was waiting for us. Without saying a word, my father touched his arm and sat in a small wooden chair beside the bed. I sat in the windowsill, grateful for the chance to melt into the wall.

Dad and the man were quiet for what seemed like a long time. Occasionally I heard my father's voice speak quickly and low. Gradually the words seemed to take on a rhythm, until they flowed, low and quiet.

I remembered what my father had said. This was once a man of great importance. When money was needed in the community, he had borrowed the money, with the expectation that the community would pay him back. Once the need had passed, the community forgot about the man. He had lost everything. He had become bitter and reclusive, and now he was ill.

I could see my father's hand on the man's arm. My father always said, "Touch people. People need to be touched." My father was telling a story. I heard the man laugh softly.

I heard my father say, "Do you remember. . . ."

The old-looking young woman came into the doorway. As the story progressed, she moved quietly across the floor, until she was sitting on the other side of the bed, holding hands with the man who must have been her father. She was smiling with her father, who reached out and patted my Dad on the knee and left his hand there.

Many hours later, sitting beside my father, I watched as the man-turned-somebody's-father closed his eyes, still touching my father, and holding his daughter's hand. He was smiling, wrapped in his star-quilt and the love of the people gathered around his bed.

In twelve-step recovery programs, men and women are invited to tell their personal stories. It is not so much storytelling as storysharing. The premise is that secret pain or struggle, kept secret, cannot be healed. To the extent that we are secretive, we inhibit growth and recovery. The key is a safe setting, and a safe community, with a strict code of ethics. Such storysharing is only done in safety. There is a vital element here. "My" story is shared with "others." "I" cease to be alone.

Political prisoners and victims of concentration camps have found similar settings beneficial. What begins as a painful opening of self in small steps leads the way for whole stories to be released. When events are shared with others, events have less control of our private lives.

While both of the above examples are not storytelling as an art form, they are storytelling at its most basic. Many people find the courage to tell their stories in other venues, impacting larger audiences, and creating other opportunities for healing. Sometimes the need to share story is the beginning of a storyteller. A storyteller is one who has empathy for the story and with those who listen. A storyteller can communicate the essence of the story from a place deep within.

At its essence, storytelling is healing, a touching of souls, and a celebration that *you are never alone.*

Preaching and Storytelling

In *Go Preach!* (Discipleship Resources, 2002; page 10), John Gilbert defines preaching:

> Preaching is a particular kind of spoken communication. It's not directed at how to make a fire or to kill a buffalo; it's not designed to find gold or to plant crops. Its intent is not to sell a product or to make a deal.
> - Preaching is the proclamation of good news.
> - Preaching is the proclamation of the word God gives us to speak.
> - Preaching is God's word uttered through human vessels.

This wonderful understanding of preaching is just as critical when we use story in sermons. Storytelling becomes a tool for preaching, but preaching has a purpose.

Storytelling is not always preaching, but preaching may be accomplished through the use of story.

I had a young friend from Africa who passed away after attending seminary in the United States. One of the most remarkable things about my friend was her ability to connect on a personal level with members of her congregation. People were naturally drawn to her, and there was such a remarkable spirit about her and a passion for those she served that it became evident she was a natural spiritual leader, gifted by God.

As a tribal person whose culture included storytelling in nearly all aspects of socialization, she tended to answer questions with a brief story. In meetings, she would encourage the group to come as close to consensus as possible, and she refrained from speaking until most people had had an opportunity to express their points of view. Children rushed to hear her tell stories in the "children's sermon" each Sunday morning. Her people, both those in Africa and those she served while in seminary, were proud of her and were honored by her leadership.

As she completed her coursework at seminary, she was required to take a class on homiletics, or the study of preaching. As she prepared her first sermon in the class, she studied the Greek text, consulted commentaries and other resources, and readied herself for the presentation. Each point of her sermon was illustrated with a story, drawn from her culture and experiences. It was her way of sharing herself.

As she finished and sat down, the professor of the class told the small crowd that they had just witnessed what a sermon was not supposed to be. The use of stories, he said, implied that one did not have enough original or creative thought. Preaching was to be an opening of the Scripture through careful reasoning and presentation. Stories were for children.

In the back of the class that day, a retired bishop, who had been visiting the campus, sat quietly. As the session concluded, the professor asked the bishop to share any comments for the students. She stood for a moment, and then responded, "I'd like to tell you a story." Warmly, she told of an event in her life and its impact on her vast ministry. When she was ready to sit down, she spoke to the young pastor. "Thank you," she said, "for reminding me that effective ministry is not choosing to impress, but choosing to touch."

Story and Exegetical Preaching

As we saw in the preaching of Jesus, a story by itself may be a sermon. We know that stories fit well in topical sermons. In Christian tradition, there is great importance placed upon the role of Scripture in worship. Exegetical preaching, the careful examination of Scripture, may seem as distant from storytelling as possible, but only if our expectation of story and of storytellers is one of entertainment. Story can reveal the intent of sacred text in a memorable way. The story itself becomes a vehicle for memory and practical application, and it has an enormous impact on a congregation. Often, a story that is consistent with the intent of the Scripture is the best choice for understanding Scripture.

In examining the role of storytelling and preaching, we wondered how effective storytelling might be in cultures that rely on technology and news bytes. From March of 2002 through December of that year the Native People's Communication Office at United Methodist Communications conducted an informal study of one hundred congregations of varying size, ethnicity, and location. We examined remembrance of key points of sermons over three different Sundays, without the knowledge of the participants. Each congregation developed a discussion group related to the pastor's sermon. The discussions took place one week after the sermon was delivered.

On a given Sunday, a small number of group members was asked to keep notes during the sermon. The remainder were to respond spontaneously. On one Sunday, the pastor preached a sermon composed of an introduction, three major points, and a conclusion. On another Sunday, the pastor developed a sermon around key points illustrated by the use of stories. On the third Sunday, the pastor chose several stories, weaving them into a conclusion. For those not asked to take notes:

- Most people could describe in detail several television shows they had watched during the week, but could not recall the Scripture used in the Sunday sermon.
- Of the sermons containing three major points, less than ten percent could recall more than one point.
- Of the sermons that utilized both storytelling and key points, a significant majority could recall the stories and the related points. Key points that were not connected to stories or anecdotes were significantly more difficult to remember.
- When storytelling became the main tool in the message, most individuals could recall all of the stories.

Although individuals who took notes could recall key points and story details, their internalization of the stories took place only upon reflection. Those who did not take notes described both the story and a series of emotional responses to the stories. They also referred to the manner in which the stories were presented by the pastor, identifying personal expressions. Most were surprised at what they recalled.

Even more interesting were observations shared by the participating pastors:

- Many found the preparation time for the telling of stories to be more extensive than the preparation of a traditional three-point message.
- Most noticed a physical response to the stories by the congregation. Congregants of all ages appeared more relaxed and paid close attention.
- Individuals responded to the pastor with specific observations regarding the stories and related key points. These comments were shared over a period of time.
- Most clergy were surprised and delighted by the number of children and youth who recalled specific elements of the message.

Some thoughts ought to spring quickly to our minds. If the human body actually slows down and relaxes while listening to story; if the human memory recalls information embedded in story at a higher level; if the story-form is one of the most successful ways of communicating with all ages; if most communication is shared through nonverbal means; if story encourages interaction on an emotional level between the storyteller and those who participate in the story—then, responsible storytelling is an incredible vehicle for sharing the Good News.

Responsible Storytelling

In many senses of the word, storytelling is an invitation to the listener to experience the story. The storyteller enters into the world of the listener by choosing an appropriate story, choosing language that relates to the listener, and offering herself up as a vehicle for the story. It is a gift that can be deeply personal, and deeply moving for both the storyteller and those entering the story.

In preaching, there are some considerations to which the storyteller must commit. Remember how the sharing of stories impacts people? Story, like music, can have a profound effect on audiences. Congregations, unlike many other audiences, are repeat attendees. We attend church because we are committed to our faith, and often to this specific faith community. Hopefully, there is a feeling of trust that develops between the pastor and those who sit in the pews every Sunday. A portion of the trust is being aware of those things that injure that trust. When we choose to use stories, we must be aware of the potential impact of the story and not manipulate that potential. Manipulating the moods of a congregation through the use of stories can create a feeling of mistrust. Any person, but especially children, may respond to the emotion of a story without being aware of what to do with that emotion. The tradition of storytellers in faith communities is not to impress but to "touch."

As speakers in congregations, we are sensitive to both the congregation and to the ministries of those who have been called and ordained to serve in ministry with us and among us. As storytellers in faith communities we are sensitive to the ongoing work of the Holy Spirit in the life of *this* community. We are responsible in our storytelling.

Reviving the First Tradition: Storytelling as Testimony

I remember two individuals who were known as storytellers but would not have considered themselves such. They in fact were survivors who had an incredible capacity to take you through events and emotions with their words and faces.

Mrs. Carroll and Tim Vanderbeek (fictitious names) never knew each other. One lived in Bellingham, Washington, and the other in Estes Park, Colorado. Both had been prisoners in concentration camps (it doesn't matter whose), one in that person's own homeland, and the other while working in a foreign country. Tim described seeing his wife in another camp, and knowing she was expecting their child. Their child was born with a mental handicap due to malnutrition, but survived to bring great joy to their family and friends. Mrs. Carroll spoke of her family and trying to survive. She did survive, and through her words brought strength to many.

What was amazing about Mrs. Carroll and Tim Vanderbeek was not just their words and the elements of their stories. They *understood* the meaning of their stories. They had thought through events and people, and from them gleaned life lessons. Within the stories for survival were characters of insight, values, courage, and joy. One sat and listened, and was pulled in. Their faces glowed as they spoke. Their bodies reflected their hearts. These were living stories contained in living persons. Each of them knew the *something* they wanted to leave with us.

In a religious sense, testimony is not just about eyewitness accounts but is an account of an individual's encounter with God. In faith communities your testimony will have value as you seek relationship with God.

There is one strong rule. Testimony must be credible. In an age when the incredible is mundane, we are called to be real. We are asked to be credible. Testimony speaks out of our humanness, or in the words of Native people, of our "real people–ness."

Testimony must be authentic. It must bleed if cut. There is nothing as un-funny as contrived humor or as plastic as feigned emotion. To be less than credible is to violate trust. As one of the most powerful means of story, testimony must be genuine.

Testimony must also be well thought through. Not all experiences or aspects of experiences should be shared in all venues. When we present human experience as story, we must have found peace with the experience, and have an understanding of what it is we wish to leave with those we pull into the experience.

Several years ago now, I buried two people significant to me: a young woman and a child. The circumstances were painful and not all of them were appropriate for an audience, even a congregation. Over the years following, I met other people who had similar stories of loss. I was able to tell them bits and pieces of my story, seldom without crying.

One Sunday morning, I was to speak in a worship service. The day before, the congregation had experienced the death of a family killed by a gunman. I had been invited as part of a service celebrating the contributions of Native Americans. At the church's request, I was wearing tribal clothing. I felt a little awkward, as I looked over the crowd. People were weeping and holding hands. The pastor spoke about the loss, and overcome with grief asked if I would speak.

As I walked to the center of the platform, I stood away from the pulpit. The story had been in my heart and mind for many years. The words were there, but I had never heard myself say them. This was the time.

In buckskins and moccasins, I told them of those that I had loved and still did. I talked about loss and days of darkness. I spoke of disbelief and confusion. Then the words came as clear to my soul as they came from my mouth. With tears running down my face, I spoke of my inability to forgive. I told them of my inability to pray. And I told them of the day when I could do both.

There is a time when we are not enough. There is a time when we have no faith, and others lend us theirs. There is a time when we realize that the presence of God surrounds us, and has all along.

Testimonies are those occasions when we say to one another, "None of us is alone." Here are some thoughts:

- Testimony need not be dramatic or profound. It does need to be honest.
- Testimony is deeply personal. If you are not given enough time to tell the story to satisfy your soul, don't tell it. Be firm.
- What is the purpose of the testimony? Know what elements are critical to the story and how you wish to present them. Storytelling through testimony must have a direction.
- While testimony can be one of the most powerful of storytelling sources, it is also the one that makes the storyteller most vulnerable. You cannot share your

story well if you are not at ease with this experience, this day. There will be other times.

- Personal experiences are initially best shared with one or two people. Look for opportunities to share them with people you trust. You will find what is important to the story and what you are comfortable sharing. From there, you may consider sharing with larger audiences.

Many churches, community centers, schools, and other venues record those who make presentations. Be certain that you are comfortable with having personal stories recorded and distributed in settings over which you have no control. You may feel at ease in sharing your story to a certain group, but not at ease with having the story shared elsewhere when you are not present. Remember, particularly in regard to testimony, more than ninety percent of communication comes not from your words but through your eyes, mannerisms, smile, stance, and body movements. In deeply personal testimony, you may wish to limit your testimony to those situations where you are physically present. Even when people indicate that recording is to further the ministry of their organization, feel at ease in saying "No." Your testimony is *your* ministry.

Wrapping Things Up

- Storytelling enables a person and a community to share what is important about themselves and their values.
- Within our stories and our languages, we preserve the essential elements that define us.
- Oral traditions predate the written word. Many early forms of literature were extensions of existing oral traditions.
- Women are usually the first storytellers we hear and are the culture bearers in many communities.
- Storytelling traditions exist in every culture of the world, each with its own unique characteristics.
- One of the major factors in the decline of storytelling was the shift from agrarian societies to industrial urban centers.
- As productivity became a measurement of human worth, there was a shift in how we valued individuals.
- World wars impacted the shape of the world economy as well as cultural values.
- As technology replaced industrialization, the need for human-to-human contact encouraged the revival of storytelling.
- The Civil Rights Movement had a secondary effect of encouraging cultural pride in many communities throughout the world. It also encouraged awareness of other cultures, including storytelling traditions.
- In biblical Middle Eastern traditions, storytellers were valuable members of society.
- Much of the Bible contains elements of oral traditions.
- Jesus was a storyteller. The Synoptic Gospels contain forty parables of Jesus.
- The telling of stories has profound physiological and psychological benefits.

- Indigenous cultures used storytelling in healing. Today, storytelling is used in healing practices as well.
- Telling our own stories offers the opportunity for growth.
- Preaching is not necessarily storytelling, but storytelling may be preaching.
- When stories are used as part of the sermon, it is easier for congregations to recall the message.
- One of the most powerful means of storytelling is personal testimony.

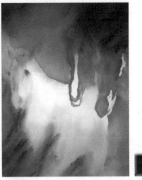

Part II
The Story

Where Do Stories Come From?

*T*he question "Which came first, the chicken or the egg?" is a little easier when it comes to storytelling. Before any storyteller rose to speak, there was a story. Someone told a tale that so moved or delighted you that you remembered it; not always in great detail, but you remembered it. You could not wait to tell someone else, and you tried to describe the story. You searched your memory for characters and plots. You reassembled them in your mind. You may not have told anyone, but you wanted to be sure of the story yourself. Finally, one day, you told the story that someone had told you. You shared your delight in the story. And the story continued.

Stories are everywhere. They are not always whole stories, but sometimes the beginnings or endings of stories. Most often, they are ideas that speak to the human condition in all of its variety.

My mother sends me pieces of stories. Sometimes they are ideas or quotations. Sometimes they are things that she observes. She has an uncanny ability to find meaning in things that others pass by. She collects them and shares them so that others might see the beauty also.

In Alaska, while shopping for groceries, my mother saw a gourd. Out of place, not only in Alaska, but also in the produce section. The gourd was large with a long neck that bent down low. At the end of the neck was an oval bulb, resembling a head. The stem was still attached. Like an abandoned swan, the gourd stood alone, proud and by itself.

As she went over to the gourd, she noticed that it was dirty. Something had damaged the outside of the green skin. It was pocked with tiny holes and warts. She brushed off the side of the gourd and placed it in her basket. As she was paying for her groceries, the clerk offered, "That's an odd-looking thing!"

When Mom got back to her little apartment, she filled the sink with warm water and washed the gourd. Drying it carefully, she placed the "bird" on an empty candle stand near the window. As the days passed, she would move the bird toward the sunlight. Autumn turned into short Alaskan winter days, and each day the gourd would be patted, touched, and gently turned.

By Christmas the bird with the bowed head had begun to shed its green skin. In thin, tiny sheets, the crisp, dried exterior began to peel away. Still resting on the candle stand, the bird-gourd was molting. People would come into the apartment and look at the gourd. Most would touch it and talk about its beautiful shape. Mom kept turning it, catching the sun.

By April, the bird-gourd was a golden brown. Standing upright on a solid base, it still rested where candles usually sit. Its sides had developed a warm patina and glow from the many touches of its admirers. Where warts and blemishes had been, there was deep texture, like a maple burl. Still, my mother turned it in the sun.

Some people called it a swan. Others a Canada goose, which flies over the Chugach Mountains in the Alaska sky. By June, it sang, seeds brushing its strong solid sides. In my mother's kitchen, the bird rested, brushed by the sun and an occasional gentle hand.

In Alaska, there was a bird, blown far from home. Bruised and tattered, it sat alone. There was one who saw the bird and took it home. Gently she turned it in the sun, willing it to fly.

The world is full of stories if we open our eyes.

I remember riding a bus from Nashville, Tennessee, to Denver, Colorado. We had made the usual obligatory stops, pausing for a moment in Kansas City. Just as we were getting ready to leave, an elderly African American woman was helped onto the bus by her daughter. Moving slowly down the aisle, and limping slightly, she touched each seat that she passed, smiling gently at each of us. Once in a while, her small hands would lift above the seats, and seemed to float in rhythmic motion.

As she passed the middle of the bus, a small boy with red hair, who had been watching her hands, said, "Is you dancin'?" She paused momentarily, smiled, and replied, "Oh, I can't dance anymore, but God gives me wings!"

Another bus at an inner-city stop.
She finds a seat and leans against the glass.
Sometimes it seems that the fare is all she's got,
But the Father knows her needs before she asks.
She remembers a time when she used to dance.
Now, it's hard to walk it seems.
She lifts her hands and says with a smile,
"Though I can't dance, the Father gives me wings!"
"He gives me wings."

Stories surround us. Rich, deep, and colorful. Stories so full of laughter they wait to burst like warm watermelon. Stories surround us that will lift our spirits and make us want to sing. There are stories in the weather, stories in the trees, stories in the animals we encounter, and stories in the people we see for only five minutes. There are stories around us every day needing to be shared.

My grandfather would say that God has hidden stars to surprise us. He delighted in cutting apple cores in half and pointing out the star-shaped places where the seeds lived. He would break a small branch of cottonwood at the joint and show me the star.

"There are starfish, and star fruit, and star anise, and stars just about everywhere," he would say. God is pleased, he believed, when we find the hidden stars.

Storytellers look for "stars" in unexpected places. It isn't that we hunt them out (although we sometimes do) but that we remain ready when we find them. We notice the small things that impact our lives, and we wish to share them.

Storytellers are remarkably generous, because stories are never personal possessions. They are meant to be given away. God must be pleased when we find the stories God has hidden for our surprise.

Stories do not need to be established or lengthy in order to be effective. A short story done well is a beautiful gift. One of the best ways to write stories, compose stories to tell, and teach storytelling is simple observation. Finding an interesting object and developing a story around it is a wonderful tool for teaching storytelling to children, as well as yourself.

On the step of a candle shop in Girdwood, Alaska, is a pair of old leather work boots. They had been worn over many years until they were soft and supple with a personality of their own. The owners of the shop had filled the boots with soil and planted flowers in them. How long the boots had been a part of the step, no one really remembered. The boots had become a soft green as moss grew over them. Around the eyelets, moss grew in gentle mounds. The old boots had become part of the environment, hosting flowers in late spring and summer, and nurturing moss in the winter. They had found a new purpose.

Sitting on the steps, drinking hot tea, I overheard a conversation between a mother and three young children: "Aren't these beautiful? Look at the flowers. Can you see the moss? How long do you think these boots have been here? Who do you think owned these shoes? Where do you think that person is now?" And then the line that made me want to jump up and hug all of them, "On the way home, let's make up a story about the boots! Okay?"

Many times, stories have come from objects that we cherish and yet pass by every day while looking for stories.

Folktales

We are all familiar with folktales. They are the stories of enchanted forests and small people with wings. There are talking animals, fish, and birds. In folktales stones speak, mountains walk, trees dance, and mermaids guide us to beautiful palaces under the sea. There are stories where children are valiant and geese lay golden eggs. Nearly every culture has folktale heroes of mammoth proportions, larger than life, who conquer evildoers (or are evildoers). Libraries are rich with collections of folktales from around the world. It is worth your while to read them and select those of particular interest to you. Here are some thoughts regarding that process:

- Most folktales came from specific cultures. Not all resources will include cultural information. Spend some time understanding the culture that gave birth to the stories. Some of the richest stories classified among folklore were designed for religious or cultural purposes. Tales from Hasidic rabbis, indigenous stories from around the world, Zen Buddhist tales, and many, many others, are more than entertainment or fantasy. They contain spiritual or cultural teachings significant to the human condition.

- Look for collections developed by storytellers. It helps to have their feedback, especially when starting out. Such resources (see Part V) will indicate things the storyteller found especially successful.
- Not all folktales were told for children. Be aware of what is age appropriate.
- As a storyteller, you may be asked to present in a variety of settings. As you look at collections, set aside stories for various occasions.
- Most historical folktales are part of the public domain, and are adaptable to a degree.
- Folktales give beginning storytellers some latitude in adaptation to accommodate learning new skills.
- If you find a collection of stories transcribed from actual storytellers, look especially for the notes regarding how the story was told, including mannerisms, props, style, and so forth. These may not be appropriate for you, but they will help you learn.
- Many libraries have video or audio recordings of storytellers. These are wonderful tools for listening and adapting styles.
- Be a student. For ideas in presentation, look at other venues of the same story: storytelling, plays, dances, opera, puppet shows, and so forth. Seeing aspects of staging helps you look at the story from different perspectives.

Literature

Literature can be a good source of material for storytelling if you are aware of the considerations. Literature is a story written by someone else for the purpose of publication. These are stories legally owned by someone else. Is it permissible to retell these stories? Sometimes, providing that the copyright allows you to do so.

Bible stories are good stories to include in your repertoire. To tell Bible stories well, it is imperative to do your homework. Know the history, setting, background, and customs surrounding a story. Seldom are original stories handed to us. Many great works of literature were based upon biblical themes. Often, there is much more than the obvious waiting within the potential of background information. Behind every Bible story is a person (or persons) waiting to be understood.

Historical literature is another excellent place to begin, as long as the resource is not historical fiction. If a story captures your interest, there are bound to be other sources to document the event. From those sources, you may develop the story in your own words and style. Don't underestimate biographies as great contributors to stories. Often, a storyteller will come across an obscure point of information that will connect with another story or lead into a new understanding.

Literature can also provide us with ideas for themes that may later develop into original stories. Sibling rivalry, betrayal, friendship, self-sacrifice, perseverance, dedication, jealousy, hope, and other relational themes can be encountered and tucked away for the future.

Other Storytellers

An elderly pastor once remarked that it was sometimes difficult to be spiritual while listening to others' sermons. When asked why, he replied, "Because one temptation that we seldom talk about is the temptation to think you could do it better."

The best way to learn storytelling is to listen to other storytellers. See how the characters shift and the face changes. Hear how the voice modulates and the words are slowed and speeded up. Sometimes you hear different ways to tell old stories. Sometimes the stories belong to the storytellers themselves and are personal.

Listening to other storytellers can make you aware of stories that may be considered public domain (available for anyone to tell). You may also discover other sources (storytellers should give credit to sources). But storytellers are also like songwriters. Stories may be a collaborative effort. You may provide the beginning, another the middle, and both of you may create an ending. More often than not, another storyteller can listen to a story you are working on creating and suggest, "Have you tried this?" Storytellers are crafters, and are usually willing and delighted to share ideas.

Listen to other storytellers as often as you are able. Attend storytelling events. Host a gathering of storytellers in your home.

Personal Experience

Testimony can be personal experience, but personal experience is not always testimony. Storytelling from personal experience is describing the events and people that have brought laughter, learning, growth, or meaning to your life. Depending on what venue you are in, personal stories may be literal truth or they may be events that have been expanded upon for the sake of story. Sometimes in preparing a story from your own experiences, characters and events from a period of several years work well in one story.

While testimony is truth, not all storytelling needs to be true. You are, after all, creating a story. Tall tales, folktales, stories derived from personal experiences, humorous stories, and even stories created to illustrate key themes may all be creations of the storyteller. You may wish to take events from your personal life and include them as part of the life of a character. You may wish to change the endings to some events. If you are storytelling in an event with the expectation of truthfulness, be credible. If you are telling a story at a festival, create good stories.

One caution: It is never acceptable to use true events from another's life without his or her permission. Period. Even disguised in a story, if your tale includes events that others will recognize as their own, seek permission or don't include them.

Creating Stories

"This is what I believe," he said.

"I believe that I am called to live in good relationship with all that is around me. I believe that I am in good relationship with the Creator. I believe that I am in good relationship with those who are my brothers and sisters, all those who are human. I believe that I am in good relationship with all Two-Leggeds, Four-Leggeds, Those that Fly in the Air, Those that Swim, and Those that Crawl Upon the Earth. I believe

that I am asked to be in good relationship with all that is created. This is what I believe."

"I believe," he said, "that if I am in good relationship with all that is around me, every act I do is a sacred act for a sacred purpose. Why would I not wish to live in good relationship with the Creator and all that is around me? This is what I believe."

"I believe," he said, "that when I gather food, it is a prayer. I believe that when I smile at someone I see, it is a prayer. I believe that when I touch a child, or feed my horse, or go to work, it is a prayer. When I make a rattle, or paint a picture, it is a prayer. When I sing, it is a prayer. When I dance, it is a prayer. When I do anything that brings joy to the Creator, it is a prayer. It is a sacred act."

"When you tell a story," I asked, "is it a sacred act; a prayer?"

His eyes lit up. "Oh yes," he said. "When I create a story, it is a sacred act. It is a prayer." He looked in my direction for a moment, and briefly caught my eye. "When you hear my story," he asked, "is it a prayer?"

We have lost the sense of the sacred in what we do. We often think of creating things that are sacred as being somber. Surely the sacred cannot be funny, or exciting, or real-people-like. That is too ordinary. The ordinary cannot be sacred. The routine cannot be sacred.

In our capacity to create, we are experiencing a gift from the Creator. When we create to give away, we are extending relationship. When we create stories, we are giving a gift, to ourselves, to others, and to God.

Not all storytellers create stories. Some people simply choose to tell stories that already exist in one form or another, and adapt them in ways that are personally appealing. But some are called to create stories.

My friend Mike DuBose is a world-class photographer. Having traveled all over the world, in peaceful and dangerous situations, Mike carries duffle bags full of equipment. He shrugs off any offer of help. He is familiar with the weight of the equipment. He knows where each piece is located. He is able to put the equipment up and take it down with precision and speed.

I have watched Mike change cameras. I have seen him wait until the light was just right, or work to create light where there was none adequate. For several hours, Mike assembled strobes along the rafters in a large gymnasium so that he could illuminate the activities at a later time. Once, while photographing a still life that involved a piece of beadwork, we sat in a darkened room. My friend allowed a small flash, held the lens of the camera open, and then flashed again. On the finished photograph, the beadwork shimmered, the colors around it pulled to their full potential of color. There was incredible skill, but also an understanding of light and darkness. Light by itself was too much. Knowing the value of darkness and the placement of light allowed us not only to keep an image but to "feel" the moment that light struck the glass beads.

There is a time each day, depending on the season, that Mike calls "golden hour." It is the time a few hours before sunset, when the amber and gold of the natural light seem to add warmth and definition to subjects and make you want to say, "Ah."

I have seen the photos of elders and children that capture the essence of a personality. I have seen rolls of film and watched Mike select the one or two photos that said exactly what he wanted to say. In slides arranged neatly in volumes are essays, poems, declarative statements, and visions.

This gift, this creative ability, this series of disciplines that go into one brief moment of capturing so much…all of this Mike calls "*making* a picture."

How does one *make* a story? You start with the basic equipment. You begin with your tools. Then, when the image is there, or the idea of an image, you apply the discipline. You work on the illumination. You work on arranging the composition. You make a story. Then, you make another.

What Makes a Good Story?

Understanding what makes a good story helps you create one. There are some clear tools to understanding a good story.

- Every strong story has a **clearly identifiable theme.** You may identify the theme at the beginning of the story, or you may choose to wait until the end. However, when the story is concluded, everyone, both you and the audience, must be aware of your intent. You may choose to weave several stories together, meeting in a common theme. Each story can be uniquely different, but the conclusion must pull them all together.
- The **plot** is the path that an individual story takes to reveal the theme. A theme without a plot is a little like a punch line without a joke. The plot may be a series of events that culminate by focusing on the theme. The plot must flow smoothly, so that those who are listening are pulled along with you through the story and not jarred by inconsistencies in the story. How you assemble the events, including which events to include in a story, may add to or detract from audience attention.
- When we think of **character development,** we think of the ways that we present the characters in our story to the audience. We want our audience to gain a visual image of each of the characters. By the end of the story, we want to have fully revealed the appropriate information about each character through the use of the plot. In addition, we want our characters to be consistent, unless behavior is to be a surprise. We reveal a great deal about our characters by the way we use voicing, mannerisms, and facial expression.
- The **style** of the story is what form(s) we use to tell the story. Is this an interactive story? Is this story narrative, or does it involve the use of dialogue?
- As we reveal the story, we create mood by using **drama**—not acting, but contrast in characters, places, descriptions, and other tools. Using the photo analogy, too much light or darkness does not create interest. The contrast between light and dark creates diversity or mood.
- The last piece of equipment is recognizing that not all audiences are alike. We do not use the same words with young children as we do with adults. In some settings, we are careful to choose the images we use as well as the theme. You might not choose to use testimony at a light-hearted event. You might be careful not to use a theme that could be uncomfortable for some audiences. As storytellers, we need to be **appropriate** for both the audience and the event.

A good story will have:
- an easily identifiable theme
- a strong plot
- strong character development
- good consistent style
- elements of drama or surprise
- appropriateness to age, setting, time, culture, and audience.

Developing Stories

When you create a story, you begin not at the beginning but at the end. You may not know the exact ending of the story yet, but the end is the focus of your work. What do you wish to leave with your audience? What is it that you want them to take home in their pockets for another day?

The theme of your story is where your heart is drawn. It is the thing that captures your attention and compels you to tell another. The theme is the thing you want your audience to remember. It is the prize won at the state fair. You have to make sure it is not too big to lug home, or too small for the ticket.

Each year at Christmas, I give a story to my brother, Rick. I will usually tell him the story on Christmas Eve before the household goes to sleep. Most often, they are not written stories. It is a shared experience between brothers.

During the course of the year, an idea for the theme will usually come to mind. Something we saw or did may inspire the thought. I make it a point not to work on the Christmas story until after Thanksgiving, so that the story will be fresh to me at Christmas. What determines the other factors in the story is the person to whom the story is to be given. What are the characters that Rick would enjoy the most? Almost always, the answer is animals. I begin to think about animals in relation to the theme. Rick knows the habits and habitats of animals, so while the animals may talk, they must be consistent with their own characteristics. That makes assigning characters a little easier. A mouse may chew on the leg of a table but probably would not move a table. A mouse and a bear could! But for the sheer sound of the words, a mouse and a moose would be even better!

What events should take place within this story? That depends on several things. Christmas is Christmas, and as much as Rick might enjoy these stories, there are cookies, and sleep, and other more important things with which to be concerned. The time frame should probably be no longer than fifteen minutes. There should be a minimum number of scenes. The language should be something Rick would understand readily.

What other factors might the story contain? We have seen that one of the traditional ways to teach values is through the use of story. What additional values should the characters demonstrate or should be revealed through the action in the story? What should the characters teach us on this journey through a story?

When we look at values within a story, we determine which values should be taught, and we pull them into the plot through characters or events. Characters may state some values outright, while others are implied through activity. At the conclusion of our story, the audience should be able to articulate the values contained in the story.

Which are the best tools to capture interest, add humor, or add drama to the story? Should the moose fly? Well, maybe, but Rick wouldn't buy it, unless it was a surprise ending. How about dance? Ah, that's a possibility. Maybe an attempt at dance. What about the mouse teaching the moose to dance? What if the near-sighted moose had to bend low, with his chin resting on the ground, watching the mouse demonstrate how to dance? Perhaps the mouse might dance in the antlers of the moose, while the moose tried to look cross-eyed over the top of his head.

We have chosen a theme and looked at appropriateness for the audience by examining the length of the story, the language, and the style. We have looked at character development and plot. We have looked at adding interest, humor, or drama.

We also need to carefully examine the images that we choose. What we say and how an audience perceives it may be two entirely different things. We use two terms to look at how stories are perceived: *explicit* and *implicit*. An explicit idea is one that may be taken at face value. The moose has antlers. All mice have tails (except those with an attraction to farmers' wives). Some ideas are implied by attitude, gesture, activity, mannerisms, or our selection of words. What is implied may be the furthest thing away from your intent, but an audience perceives it. You may say, "The moose had antlers." As you say those words you may extend your arms to the size of antlers, widen your eyes, and nod your head. You have just said that the moose had *enormous* antlers. If you shudder, you convey that the moose had not only enormous but *fearsome* antlers. If you shake your head sadly and look forlorn, you have cast a value judgment on the respectability of antlers.

More than any other stories that we might use, a story we create allows us to be ourselves. It reflects our interests and our values. Creating a story enables us to share with others those things that cause us delight. More than that, creating a story is an extension of who we are, a sharing of ourselves in a unique way, and a contribution to the body of stories from which others may draw.

Storytelling or Drama?

Storytelling is the conveying of ideas through the use of story. It is a face-to-face communication between the storyteller and the audience. Most often, while the ideas are established, stories are not memorized word by word. By the time a story is told, whether it is an original story or a borrowed one, the storyteller has adapted the story to fit his or her personality and comfort. The story may be adapted to fit a particular audience and time frame. The story itself may be altered or changed in the middle of a telling to adjust to a particular audience. Tools may be incorporated to fit a specific venue. Audience members may participate at the storyteller's request. Most often the storyteller is alone. There may be dialogue and character differentiation, but the storyteller assumes the roles of all characters. The personality of the storyteller is an integral part of storytelling in the selection, presentation, and audience contact of the story. The audience and the storyteller interact.

Drama historically is an extension of storytelling, but drama and storytelling have evolved into different art forms. Drama has a prepared script, and actors rehearse the script, along with movement suggestions, props, set, and direction of the performance.

The script is memorized, and in repeated performances the integrity of the play is maintained according to the direction given in rehearsal. Actors most often do not have face-to-face contact with the audience, even if house lights are raised. The audience members are not participants but observers of the interaction occurring between characters. While much of an actor's experience, personality, and characteristics go into developing a character, the function of acting is not the revelation of self in human contact.

One-person dramatic performances may include elements of the contact between a storyteller and an audience, but they still rely on the script. What is essential in storytelling is a recreating of the story each time it is told. It is making the story live to each group of people that hears the story. Stories that require extensive memorization prohibit the storyteller from the free use of interaction and adaptation in the communication of the story.

While storytelling is oral communication, it is the oral communication of images rather than specific words. The storyteller is a weaver of images.

Ownership

A short while back at a national gathering, I heard a speaker tell a moving story about an incident that occurred when he was a young man. It was the kind of story that brought laughter and tears. It was an effective conclusion to a long day of training.

A young man sitting next to me had a small assemblage of books near his chair. He acted a bit puzzled, and started looking through one of the books. Quietly, he handed me a book by an internationally known author. While the crowd was congratulating the speaker on his presentation, I read the passage that my friend had opened before me. There, almost word for word, was the same story. It involved the same city, the same names, and the same events. The author was twice the age of the speaker, and the event, according to the book, had probably occurred when the speaker was in grade school.

Over the period of a few months, I heard the speaker recount the same wonderful story. People began to request it, and he gladly shared the story in setting after setting. I often imagined that in every crowd, someone else had read the same book, and wondered why he was making this beautiful story his own.

Public speaking is not like writing. We imagine that we are speaking before this crowd only. We hope that this story or illustration will be effective this one time. We have all heard clergy use the same story, told in first-person, until it becomes accepted. With the advent of sermon-of-the-month clubs, and other professional publications for speakers, it is easy for thousands of people to obtain the same presentation in the same context.

There are also other legitimate reasons for what may sound like the same stories. People from the same cultures or language groups may have common experiences or use common word illustrations. Some experiences may also have greater likelihood of being duplicated because of similar circumstances.

Many Lakota or Dakota people that I know have grandparents who referred to animals as "people," or the "mouse-people," "deer-people," or other personifications.

These are based on cultural and theological concepts. They are not individual expressions. Colloquial expressions, such as "Bless your heart" or referring to one's brother as "Bubba," do not have individual ownership. We expect that there will be many uses of cultural or colloquial expressions or illustrations. What we need to be concerned with is respecting those who have gone before us. Ethics asks of us that we conduct ourselves in appropriate ways.

Respecting the Storyteller Before You

There are three wonderful storytellers that I travel to hear whenever I am able. One, a Maori from New Zealand, has the ability to tell stories from his own tradition as well as from other traditions around the world. His voice changes intensity and texture with ease, and time passes so quickly that before you are settled, his stories have concluded. Another, Eastern Cherokee and Irish, has a style that combines the best Native traditions with the folk styles of the Smoky Mountains. A creator of stories, she moves from character to character, changing voices and expressions with great insight. The third is, by profession, a farmer from North Dakota who speaks naturally and comfortably. In the same voice as he might greet you, his personal and traditional stories wrap warmly around you, and you feel pulled into the experience and enriched.

Three different people, with different styles—each possessed with natural ability and a love for people that urges them to share from their spirits. There is something else about each of them. They have a deep respect for the storytellers who have gone before them and will follow after them. Traditional stories are told in a respectful manner. They are told with the permission of their people, and in ways that honor their people. Personal stories are shared with openness. Stories from other cultures, when told, are told with the cultural sensitivities of the cultures from which the stories came. We are keepers of tradition, and we honor those traditions by respecting them. We respect even those traditions that are not our own.

Other Traditions: Respecting the Culture

Among many Native people groups, tribal stories are shared within the tribal circle. If a story is to be shared outside of the tribal circle, then permission is asked of those who keep the traditions. We do not profit from the things that belong to our people. There are many stories that are only told in religious settings. These are not told out of those settings.

Over the years, I have heard many wonderful stories. Some are tribal, and some are personal. Some are true, and would be wonderful to tell or write. Some, if written, would sell large numbers of books. When I have encountered these wonderful stories, I have encouraged those to whom they belonged to tell them or write them or to enlist the help of others in the process. I have encouraged them sometimes over a period of years. Other than that, I have treasured the memory of those stories, but I have never repeated them.

Personal stories, like songs, belong to individuals. Sometimes a song or story is given as a gift, and one becomes the bearer of the song or story. At the time of death, a family may give a story belonging to the deceased to another, who continues the story by telling it. There is a joke among Native people that we may "talk about" each other, but we never tell each other's stories.

As a rule, Native people are reluctant to share stories from other cultures without permission. Hopis seldom share Haida stories. Choctaws do not tell Ojibway tales. Unless we are acquainted intimately with another culture, we are careful about taking a story that may have been written for another context.

Often, collections of stories from other cultures are simply that, collections of stories. For what purpose were these stories written? Are those traditions still practiced today? Did the author of this resource use them with the permission of those to whom these stories have meaning? Can we, as storytellers, adequately tell this story, while offering respect to the storyteller who has gone before?

When we look at Zen stories, Hindu tales, Polynesian folk stories, Aboriginal creation stories, Irish myths, stories from Hasidic rabbis, or other great stories, we need to do our homework. We need to ask.

Sometimes, stories from antiquity pose no cultural questions of great degree. Sometimes stories from other cultures have no connection to traditions, but were simply entertaining. We need to know. Collections of stories assembled by storytellers are often more detailed in regard to history and style. Both in our storytelling and in collecting stories, we need to respect those who first told these stories.

Biblical Stories

The Bible is perhaps one of the world's greatest sources for stories. Within the Old Testament alone is an incredible volume of resources for storytellers. Bible stories, however, are not for the faint of heart. There are stories of murder, incest, rape, war, world destruction, slavery, jealousy, revenge, trickery, sorcery, genocide, prostitution, self-sacrifice, love, bravery, ritual, adventure, romance, songs, poetry, devotion, courage, and hundreds of other themes. Not all biblical stories are meant for all audiences or age groups. The Bible is a collection of stories revealing God's great love for humanity. The people in the Bible are all too human.

There is also within Bible stories the promise of hope, renewal, relationship with God, inclusion with those who believe, and overwhelming love. As those who tell Bible stories, we must believe that there is more than just story. We must believe that we are participants in changing lives. We are reminded each time we tell a story that this message speaks to us as well. We are people of The Story.

There is a courtesy in the way that most storytellers treat sacred text—any sacred text. What is considered sacred by people ought to be treated with respect.

Many Bible stories do not contain great detail. Many of the parables of Jesus are short, a mere few sentences on a page. How do we tell Bible stories and remain respectful?

Here are some thoughts:
- Don't rewrite the text. Bible stories require some of the most extensive preparation. Understand what the story is saying to the best of your ability. Be true to the text.
- In many contemporary children's stories, Bible stories are expanded to include

"it might have happened" themes. If you choose this style, make certain that it is understood you are not telling "a Bible story" but a story related to a biblical event.

- An effective tool for expanding on a biblical theme is to create a story or choose a personal or existing story in which the text may be included without altering it. Make certain that the theme of your story is consistent with the message of the text.

- Just as in historical stories, it is acceptable to use historical and cultural information in story form to illuminate the Bible story. For example, it is important in the parable of the good Samaritan for people to understand the historical conflict regarding the Samaritan people. You might begin, "Children were told if they could not say anything good, not to say anything at all. So, no one talked about the Samaritans. . . ." In a couple of phrases you have identified the fact that no one really liked Samaritans and that this feeling was being culturally passed down.

- Age appropriateness is important in Bible-story telling. You can be true to the message of the text, but understand that not all age groups will understand all concepts or be able to handle all events. The birth of Jesus is a beautiful story full of remarkable images, but young children might not be ready to process the murder of children in Bethlehem by Herod's soldiers.

- If you "take away" something from the biblical story, do so only if it does not alter the message of the story. You may describe evident emotion. Don't feel the need to add characters or events that are not in the text. Storytelling in this regard is honoring the tradition of the story.

Who Owns a Story?

Scary Story #1: We all have at least one horror story. I don't mean the kind you use to frighten children out of their marshmallows. I mean the kind of story you would just as soon forget, but need to remember so that someone else can avoid the pitfall.

I have a personal story that I have only told twice in my life. Like most of my stories, it is true. It really is about my grandmother, and since she is no longer living, I hesitate to share the story frequently. One day, it was appropriate to tell the story to a group of professional people, and I shared this important, true story.

In Kansas City, six months later, I had the opportunity to speak to a large gathering. After the event, a kind woman came up to me and shook my hand, commenting, "I heard the story about the grandmother a few months ago." She mentioned the name of a storyteller who had been at the earlier event. She said, "He did say that he had heard the story from someone else, but didn't say the name. Was it your grandmother or his?"

I was a little uncertain how to proceed, so I simply let it go. I was also disturbed because the story was so personal that I seldom told it.

Another six months later, a slightly altered version of my story appeared in a magazine. Someone who had been in Kansas City had written the story. Because the story was so personal, I spoke to the editor of the magazine, who made a call to the writer, who retracted the story with some effort.

As a result I copyrighted the story and wrote it for a children's book, even though it had not been my wish. It seemed the only way that I could control the use of a beautiful story that was so personal.

Who owns a story? Morally, it is the people group who gave the story birth, or the person who created the story. Legally, it is the person who holds the copyright.

If we tell a story that belongs to another, it is imperative to ask that person or that group for permission. That a story is told in a public setting does not mean that a story is public material. Most often, it has nothing to do with monetary issues. It has to do with how an individual feels about something he or she has created. Many times, people will simply say, "Yes, I'd be honored."

It never detracts from a story to indicate the source. Not only does it prevent mis-understandings, but it also helps establish you as a person of credibility. Your style, your voice, your presence will make the story unique. Imagine an actor not acknowledging the playwright. When you give credit to the originator of a story, you are also giving a gift to your audience.

There may be times when you choose a story in the public domain that you wish to alter. You may choose another ending, or change the gender of a character. You may make human characters into animals or change an element of the plot. You are doing something creative! It is always appropriate to say, "This story is an adaptation of ____. I've made some changes to the original story, which has always been one of my favorites." You are acknowledging the original work, and letting the audience know that there are some changes.

You may choose to combine elements from several stories. Make use of the time that you spend acknowledging the other works by helping your audience look at tools of storytelling. You might say, "Sometimes several stories have parts that are just too good to pass up. What if we combined them into something new?"

Finally, trust your deepest instincts. Have you ever looked in a catalog and seen an item of clothing on a model that was beautiful? Be content with allowing others to be beautiful. A wonderful, original story is sometimes best told by its creator. Be assured of your gifts and delight in the gifts of others.

Copyrights: When Laws Have Priorities

Written stories may be copyrighted. Even unpublished stories can be registered with the U.S. Copyright Office. Most copyrights protect the creator against others using the story in any fashion without permission, including copying in whole or in part. Most copyrights also prohibit the public performance of a work for profit. Some prohibit the public performance of a work, period. Most children's resources allow the book to be read publicly. Know the restrictions on any copyrighted work. You can count on the fact that if you don't someone else will.

It is not always permissible to record storytellers. Ask first. Never let anyone record your storytelling if it is original work until it has been copyrighted. Many people from indigenous cultures would prefer that you not record their stories. It is important to ask them. It is also a good idea not to use someone else's stories unless they have been copyrighted and you give proper credit. Protect other people in the same way that you would wish to be protected.

We do our best work when we are creating something to give away. Do everything you are able with the spirit of generosity. Protect what you create, so that you are able to share it with as many people as possible. Copyrighting your work helps to protect it from those who would take advantage of your work. Copyrighting also allows you to give permission to others who have good ideas for sharing your work.

One of the greatest blocks to creativity is fear. As you eliminate unnecessary fear, you are able to live generously and give freely. That giving is what storytelling is all about.

Part III
The Storyteller

The Pool

*T*here once was a pool of water that rested between two low hills. If you stood near the pool you could see the Great Ocean in the distance, and if you stretched very high you could see Long Man, the river, as he flowed into the ocean.

Near the pool was Old One, an ancient scrub oak with knurled branches and twisted trunk. But he did not speak, except when the wind blew through his leaves and they fluttered together. All was quiet around the pool. If one listened carefully, one could hear the sound of the Great Ocean and Long Man as he hurried to the sea.

Quietly the pool rested. Only the Wind disturbed her stillness, causing ripples on her surface. On warm days, she would catch the reflection of Father Sun and be bright like a shiny stone. When the Loud One would speak and make rain, she would be dark and thoughtful. Occasionally, at least once a year, Old One would toss her a leaf, as if to say "Are you still there?" The leaf would float gently on her surface and come to rest in the grasses on her banks.

People would come to the pool. The Two-Leggeds and Four-Leggeds came. In the early morning and early evening, the Four-Leggeds would come softly as if afraid to make a sound. They would pause awhile, bend down, and drink some of the water from the pool. Some would step briefly inside the pool and let her water touch them. They would stop awhile and then leave. Sometimes a Two-Legged would come, often alone, but sometimes in pairs. They would sit in the grass near her banks and watch the pool. Sometimes they, too, would step inside of her and sigh deeply. Often they would bend low and dip a hand into the pool and taste the cool water. The pool did not mind. She liked the company.

When the days became long and Warm Wind blew across the two hills, the pool sat quietly. In the distance she could hear Long Man as he rushed along. She thought, "How small I am." Old One on the hill cast his mighty shadow across the pond, and she felt insignificant. And when Grandmother Moon had chased Father Sun from the sky, the pool felt small, alone, and unimportant. Even the Stars reflected in her surface did not cheer her.

The Dawn found the pool very still. Dancing and flitting just above her, the Dragonflies felt sadness. The Four-Leggeds who came each day did not pause as long, and when the Clouds covered Father Sun, the Old One (even though it was not his time) *threw a leaf onto the pool to see if she was all right. When Grandmother Moon had chased Father Sun from the sky once again, the pool was dark and still.*

As Darkness lay down to cover the Hills, the Wind blew through the Old One's leaves, and the Old One told the Wind. The Wind playing with the Great Ocean told the Ocean, and the Ocean told Long Man. Long Man told the Trees along his banks, and the Trees told the Ones Who Fly. The Ones Who Fly told the Four-Leggeds, and the Four-Leggeds told the Two-Leggeds. And when Father Sun had sent Grandmother Moon to her lodge, standing on the banks of the pool was the Ancient of Days.

"Ho, daughter," the Ancient of Days began, "I have come to speak with you." The pool was still. "Why is your heart sad?" the Ancient of Days asked. The pool barely rippled. The hand of the Ancient of Days brushed the surface of the pool, and the pool's heart was softened. "I have rested here all my days," she began. "I do not crash and roar like the Great Ocean. I cannot run like Long Man. I cannot see long distances or stand strong like the Old One. I can only reflect the Clouds or the Stars. The Four-Leggeds come, but they do not stay. The Two-Leggeds come, but they do not speak. No one calls my name, because I have done nothing to earn one. I am a pool. A small pool." And with that, the pool became dark again.

The Ancient of Days began to laugh, and then stopped suddenly. The eyes of the Ancient of Days softened. "Oh, daughter, pool!" The voice was soft. "The Great Ocean roars. That is its purpose. Long Man runs. That is what he must do. Old One stands strong. That is the way of trees. But you. ..." the voice became almost a whisper, "You are the place of deepness. You are the cold water that gives Life. You are the place of rest. You are stillness from the roar. You are peace from the running. You are the place where one need not speak. You have a name! It is The Place Where One Runs To!"

The surface of the still water rippled and if water can sing, it sang! It caught the light from Father Sun and sent it back again. It surged deep and cold. Deep within itself, the pool was happy.

And the Ancient of Days sat down and stayed awhile.

> *Creator,*
> *The distance of my vision is small.*
> *Yours is large.*
> *I can see only what is around me,*
> *and behind me.*
> *You know what I am,*
> *and what I will be.*
> *Name me.*
> *Define me.*

My Native traditions teach me that we are all connected. The Lakota phrase is *Mitak(q)ue Oyasin,* meaning "all my relations," or "we are all related." All of our lives have the potential for relationship. We have the potential for relationship with

God. We have the potential for relationship with those around us. We have the potential for relationship with all of Creation.

We are connected to each other in ways we do not see. We are connected to our neighbor and to the person who checks us through the grocery line. We are connected to the person we see for only a few minutes on the bus, the dog down the road, and the child in the next town.

We are connected with those who extend love to us, and even with those who would do us harm. We do not choose those who come in contact with our lives, but we choose how we will respond. That is where being the in-all-the-world-there-is-no-one-like-me person is so vital. We are not asked to identify the thing in our life that might be useful to someone else. We are asked to be willing to extend relationship wherever possible.

Spirit, Mind, and Faith

In the entire world there is no one like you. No one. No one speaks like you. No one smiles exactly the way that you do. No one has your exact experiences. In the entire world, there is no one like you.

I once heard a beautiful sermon on giving our talents, *our best,* to God. God wanted the things that I could do well. Later in the day, my father said, "You remember the sermon?" I nodded. "I don't think it is exactly like that," my father said. I listened, waiting for more. "I believe," my father said, "that God especially wants our worst. We're all pretty good at sharing the things we are proud of. God wants us to give God the things we think nobody wants."

In 2 Corinthians 4:7 there are words of hope for the imperfect among us: *But we have this treasure in clay jars, so that it may be made clear that this extraordinary power belongs to God and does not come from us.*

This is not a passage dealing with excusing ourselves from excellence but a reminder that in all we do for God there is an element of the "other than," a promise that as we are willing, God uses us in ways we could not have imagined.

While we are confident in the things we do well, most of us secretly compare ourselves to others and see the things we believe are our shortcomings. Sometimes it is precisely the things we view as our shortcomings that may be the most endearing to other people and the most useable by God. There are millions who have wonderful gifts, but few who willingly offer "themselves." It is not always about talent. Sometimes it is about being prepared and being willing.

In the entire world, there is no one like you. In all that you do, and especially in storytelling, the spirit and the mind of the storyteller enter into every story. More than the selection of the story itself, the essence of the storyteller, himself or herself, will determine the effectiveness of the storytelling moment.

The Role of the Spirit

Later, we will talk about storytelling as an event. We think about storytelling as preparing for the event, the event itself, and after the event. In all areas of storytelling, the spirit of the storyteller is a critical factor. Behind the words, beyond the plot of the story, is the person that you are. Remembering that is one of the most important things that you will ever do.

Scary Story #2: I had the wonderful opportunity of speaking at a Eucharistic Congress in celebration of the year of Jubilee. Over several days, I was able to speak with priests, nuns, and other American Catholics employed by the church and its institutions.

On a personal level, I was moved and challenged by the many dedicated people I met, and by the uplifting conversations between events. As others shared their faith journeys with me, my spirit was encouraged.

There was no television or telephone in my room, so in between workshops, I walked, prayed, read, or was grateful for genuine silence.

About ten thousand youth came for a Saturday event that overlapped the workshops and the other activities. I had been asked to tell a story to the youth gathering. The event was outside. On either side of the stage was a large screen showing the image of the person at the microphone. For an hour before me, there had been a music concert, with nationally known groups, and vibrant Christian rock music. As the last group finished a final guitar chord, the emcee stepped to the microphone and introduced me. Television and professional video cameras were scanning the crowd. Groups of young people, excited by the presence of cameras and energizing music, were jumping up and down and cheering as the television crews passed by them.

I started to tell a story, but could only get out a few sentences before the cheering would begin as the cameras panned the crowd. I couldn't hear myself through the monitors, and my voice echoed again and again through the crowd. The young people were still dancing from the music. I looked over at the emcee and others who were standing just off to my right. The expressions on their faces said, "What can we do about it?" At the top of my voice, with little expression or emotion, I finished the story and walked from the stage. I went back to my room wandering why I was there.

The next day, I was to speak in the same setting to an even larger crowd. I lay awake much of the night wondering what to do. I did not have a loud voice even with a state-of-the-art public address system. I was not an entertainer, or a high-power speaker. The stories I told were simple and true, not always wonderfully entertaining or dynamic.

I went to breakfast and found a table by myself in the corner of the room. An elderly nun asked if she might sit down. With both hands warming on her cup of tea, she began to tell me how various parts of my story the day before had meaning for her. She finished by saying, "You were here for me."

Whenever I would leave for a journey, my Dad would always end his farewell remarks by saying, "Remember who you are." It didn't mean one thing in particular. It meant the sum total of who I was, who I wished to be, and from where I had come.

I could hear the music coming from outside. In my suitcase was my tribal clothing from an earlier part of the trip. I prayed. I showered to remind myself of new beginnings. I put on my moccasins, leggings, shirt, jewelry, and robe. Standing in front of the mirror in my quiet room, I unbraided my hair and brushed it into its full length. I put sweetgrass oil at my hairline and temples.

I asked if I might walk rather than ride in the golf cart to the front of the crowd. The last musical group was finishing their final set. The emcee said something over the noise of the crowd, but I couldn't hear it. I walked up the steps of the stage, and walked what seemed the longest distance I had ever taken. Looking across the crowd, I saw people moving about, talking, and still responding to the music. Every now and then a cheer would lift up. I said a prayer, my hundredth of the morning.

I removed the microphone from the stand and walked to the center of the stage. I begin to sing. Not loud, but soft. I closed my eyes, feeling the wind blowing through my hair. I sang the words for a new day. I sang of renewal and joy. I sang a song sung by those who had come before me. When I was done singing, I opened my eyes. The screens on either side showed my face. Youth and adults stood quietly, eyes fixed on the center of the stage. "This is my story," I heard myself say.

"Remember who you are." Not what you feel circumstances compel you to be, but *who you are*. No one in the entire world is like you. Know your spirit and why you are there.

Know not only who you are, but also who you are not. Be the best you. In the end, that is what will be the most effective.

Spirit. It is such an unusual word. It describes enthusiasm. It describes intensity. It describes a need to communicate the importance of what you are saying. It also describes the manner in which you do all of the above.

There is not a technique to teach you to be passionate about what you do. There are ways to assist a person in overcoming the obstacles to sharing himself or herself. But first, there must be that desire. The word *amateur* implies that one is doing something for the sheer love of it. In that case, I hope that we all, as storytellers, remain amateurs. I hope that we share story because of the love of it.

There is a place where deer dance. There must be many of them scattered around in hidden places that we don't often see. But they are there.

There is a place called Grouse Mountain, near Lake Chelan, in Washington State. My father would take us there, each autumn, when frost clung to the ponderosa pines and apple cider stands sprung out of the earth and settled along roadways.

We would drive away from the noise and bustle of other cars to Grouse Mountain. We would eat canned salmon and baked beans out of their cans and listen to the owls and grouse. It was here that my father showed us a path worn deeply into rock by centuries of migrating herds of deer and elk. It was a place of wonder and awe.

We had walked a rather long distance. I had sat to rest on a rock, while my father walked a few paces further around a bend in the trail. Out of the corner of my eye, I saw my father motion with his hand, calling me to come over. We did not talk often in the woods. It seemed an irreverent thing to do.

Through a close growth of pine, juniper, and fir, my Dad parted the branches, letting them fall back without bruising them. There was a clearing, surrounded by fallen logs. In the middle of the woods on Grouse Mountain was an amphitheater, made by wind, rain, and the weight of heavy snow. My father leaned over the logs and pointed to the ground. The grass had long since been worn away. In the heart of the clearing was a collage of hoof prints, lying over each other in random pattern, as if one wanted to outdo the others.

Together the two of us climbed a short distance away and lay quietly on the mountainside in the midst of some friendly rocks. The moon came out and brightened the sky, reflecting off the rocks, grasses, and others things, which welcomed it by turning their light colors skyward.

Quietly, they came. Ears standing up, they paused occasionally, eating their way down the mountainside. Some moved on down the mountain, but some stayed, filling the clearing. In the moonlight, last spring's fawns began to play, leaping at each other and running in circles. Occasionally, older does would join in, while some stood watch. In the moonlight, deer were dancing for the sheer joy of it.

As the deer moved on, we did too, returning to our canned salmon and baked beans. We had been observers, caught up in a celebration of exuberance. There on a mountainside we had wandered happenstance onto another's place of joy. It was The Place Where Deer Dance.

Have you ever watched a child dance? Jumping, skipping, leaping, turning, the child shows sheer joy, in both the music and the need to respond. What is beautiful about the dance? Discipline will come later. Technique will make the movements more fluid. Practice will add control. What is beautiful is the spirit of the dance. If we are fortunate, when the discipline, technique, and practice offer more alternatives, the spirit will remain.

As a storyteller, treasure the thing inside of you that makes you want to share not just stories, but especially *this story.* You will know it. It may be a story you found or one you created. You will want to share this thing. Why? Because it affected you. After you have told the story many times, and found better ways to tell it; after you have identified phrases and key words that make the story sing; after all of this, the story will do something for you still.

You can tell the difference. A skater executes a flawless performance. The choreography is beautiful. The jumps are timed with precision. Everything is in place. Another skater takes the ice. Her body movements do not just fit the music, they express the music. Hands seem to not just lift but to *reach toward you.* The jumps are flawless, but they also make you feel as if you had executed the jump yourself. You are moving with the skater. When the music is complete, there is emotion left hanging in the air. It is spirit.

Faith and the Storyteller

Is there a difference in storytelling in the faith community? Yes, in many ways there are significant differences. Primarily we need to look at two areas:
- the purpose and role of stories in communities of faith; and
- the faith of the storyteller.

As we saw earlier, storytellers in any traditional community serve as culture bearers. Within our stories are contained elements of our cultures that we wish to transmit to other generations. Our primary purpose is not to entertain but to continue culture. Storytellers in faith-based communities share that same purpose. We are sharing the stories, and creating stories, that contain the essence of what we believe. Our primary purpose is to share and continue our faith. There is a reason why we tell stories, and a reason why we tell the stories we do.

There is also a reason why we choose storytelling as a vehicle of culture. Storytelling is personal contact. The sharing of faith at its best is personal. Storytelling is an effective means of communication for both large and small groups, as well as for multi- or single-generational audiences. Though we have moved away from it to a degree, sharing our faith through the use of story is one of our earliest traditions.

Storytelling in communities of faith serves a teaching function. The storyteller must be accurate to the source and, in many cases, to the tradition. The storyteller then becomes a scholar (at the very least, a dedicated student) of her or his faith and its tradition. To a larger degree, the storyteller becomes an interpreter of that faith.

As storytellers in faith communities we must know our cultures, be careful in how we interpret those beliefs through story, be accurate to our sources, and inspire faith.

There is also another important ingredient. We must believe. We must be credible in our personal faith.

Would you allow me to be personal for a moment? When I was younger I did not feel comfortable with the designation "storyteller." A good portion of those feelings came from the extraordinary storytellers I knew. To me, stories had a sacred function, and people who shared them were larger than life. Storytellers were heroic. I am not exactly certain that they would have called themselves storytellers. They would have been comfortable with "culture bearers" or "keepers of tradition." Modesty would have prevented them from assuming a claim to any skills or accomplishment. They were story-keepers.

In Lakota tradition, individuals were granted the right to tell stories because they embodied the values of that particular story in their own lives. They were, and are, living stories.

Most of the stories I tell are true. That is a prejudice on my part, because the people I have known have been remarkable people. When I tried to talk with others about the people who have impacted my life, I was telling their stories. As I have spoken about them, certain aspects of their lives and characters have become solidified in my thinking. Hindsight also gave me the ability to see the movement of God in my life through other people. As I spoke the words about their lives, the values they had taught me became clearer. Each time that I "spoke those beliefs into being" my life changed as I shared the stories of others.

There was also another unsuspected thing that took place. As I shared the words and the experiences, they impacted my life to such a degree that I made conscious decisions to commit to many of those same beliefs. Stories had become an opportunity for spiritual growth. I not only believed but also was practicing those beliefs. I was affirming the legacy of faith. The discipline of sharing stories enabled me to look at my own life experiences as a story. I was startled by the many answered prayers, the orchestration of events, and the unmistakable reality of God in my life. I prayed more. I observed more. I celebrated the lives of others more. And I looked for God in unexpected places.

I had become part of The Story.

When we engage the stories that are part of our traditions, like all others before us, they have the power to impact our lives. The difference is, we live in them. We wrap them around ourselves and become warm. We share that warmth. There is not a way to step into the water of faith stories without becoming wet. When we do step in, it challenges our faith, our commitment, and the way we choose to live. It is supposed to.

Here, I believe, is why. Remember when we talked about the story as a living being and said that when it touches the spirit of another, a story lives? It is the potential impact of a story. It is the potential for uplifting someone, for offering hope or empowerment. Here is an essential element of my faith. When we encounter spiritual truth, whether in a story or in a casual conversation, we encounter the Living God, ready for relationship. At every turn, we discover God. We do not cause it. It happens because we are willing to tell the story. Someone meets God.

Is the Spirit of God present with us when we tell stories of faith? I believe so. With all my heart, I believe so. Is the Spirit of God with us only as we share stories of faith? No, with all my heart I believe that the Spirit of God delights in revealing God in surprising places and blessing our lives in all that we do. Still, for clergy and laity, young and old, formally educated and life-student, there is a desire to tell *The Story.* At times, the testimonies of those who have gone before us and the presence of God seem tangible, and the words flow beyond our capabilities. Someone listens and hears with new ears. There is an anointing of those who tell stories and those who sing and those who bake bread and give it away. We are rediscovering those things.

When I was younger, I was not comfortable with being called a storyteller. Now I am older, and even more so than when I was young, I stand in awe at the power of stories. I am not willing to be called a storyteller, for I am still a student. But I cannot stop, for there is much to tell and so many reasons to do so. I am one who heard *The Story,* and it changed my life. I cannot stop telling others about it.

The Making of a Storyteller

What makes a good storyteller? There are a number of variables. Some are the product of upbringing. Some have to do with talents and gifts. Most are learnable and may be developed.

Common sense helps us identify some basic qualities of a good storyteller. Good storytellers, like most artistic people, will have a desire to tell stories. They may tell jokes or recount adventures or misadventures. Some will be serious. Some will be funny. In many indigenous communities, adults will watch for children who answer questions with story, or a prolonged well-thought-through account. Most of these children will have a gift for memory and be inquisitive.

As we have seen, in some cultures, the role of storyteller is hereditary, passing from parent to child. Most of these cultures also have observed that there are others who seem to possess both talent and memory, and they have made exceptions to the rule of heredity. What we can draw from these cultures is that children surrounded by those who tell story learn early to think in an orderly fashion, and they recount events and images by the telling of stories. There are those who are naturally gifted and, if taught the discipline of thinking in story and recounting stories, become the greatest storytellers.

As part of a small gathering of storytellers near Santa Fe, New Mexico, in August of 2002, I asked the question one evening, "What makes you a good storyteller?" There were some professional storytellers, some educators, five traditional Native storytellers, one Australian Aboriginal teller of Dreamtime tales, an Ainu culture bearer, and several college-age observers. As each member felt comfortable speaking, she or he spoke. Everyone agreed on two things. All could not escape the fascination with both listening to and telling stories. All also agreed that being recognized as a storyteller was not a designation one gave oneself, but rather a recognition made by one's community. In essence it was other people who recognized that an individual was a storyteller. In some cases, the right to tell stories was granted from a specific community. As storytellers, we are "called out" by our communities.

Another interesting point became evident. Without exception, all of these storytellers were primarily listeners. If we had to place a contemporary Western label on them, most of these storytellers were introverts rather than extroverts. That is not to say that in that group of people there were not those who were "hams." All had gifts of public performance, but through personality or discipline they were not attention grabbers or those who sought approval by public acceptance. They laughed easily, teasing one another and responding both physically and vocally to the stories told.

Almost all were avid readers. They stressed the importance of experiencing "words" in a variety of voices.

As observers of the world around them, the small group was sensitive to the subtleties of life and story. They borrowed from one another and gave to one another. They had cultivated the use of memory, each relying on different tools or skills.

I had recently watched a television program on the training of high-level law-enforcement officers. In the film, they had allowed the trainees to enter a room for a brief period of time, and then led them away. Relying only on what they had been able to observe, the trainees described in detail everything that was in the room and how it was arranged. As storytellers we rely on instinct, sensitivity, and visual memory.

In our modern, fast-paced society, we train ourselves to deaden our senses to some degree. We can talk on the phone and watch television at the same time. Instead of listening for night-noises, we drown the occasional sounds with white noise. In our cars, music and audio books make the traffic and rush less imposing. In crowds, we are not as sensitive to those around us as we might be in intimate settings. Good storytellers create a world that is sensory. In order to do that we intentionally alter the way we experience the world.

My brother and I share life with an older female Chinese Shar-pei. Her vision and hearing have deteriorated, and her arthritis makes it difficult to walk. She has buck-teeth, so eating is a hit-and-miss endeavor, and she is overweight. In short, she is the perfect reflection of the rest of us. Her name is Winter Moon.

Winter Moon commands respect, and we all know our places. She knows all of the trees in the neighborhood, and insists on stopping at each one to "check her messages." She plays with two Alaskan ravens. They take turns chasing each other and are sad when it is time to go in. What Winter Moon cannot see, she touches. She rubs her face over flowers and leaves, the sensitive skin registering something I cannot see. She can tell by the sound when a child or animal is in distress, and she cries until someone comes to check. She senses moods, and comes close to lie near by. Hers is a world of delicate sensibilities.

There is a tendency for me to view my world as more sophisticated than hers. And yet, when I am careful about observing the world and listening to another soul, my sensibilities shift from multitasking to experiencing the world in much the way Winter Moon does. Relax; the ravens refuse to play with me. I am just not worth chasing. If I let the world touch me, if I listen to the subtleties of distress or joy, if I move closer when I am needed, then I experience the world differently. But I have to choose to do all of those things before I can experience them.

How do we make those experiences into story?

Preparing Yourself for the Story

My brother has severe learning disabilities and has always found reading difficult and spelling impossible. Sitting at my computer I showed him how he could type in a word and check the spelling. Of course, his reply was, "How does the computer know if it is spelling the word right?" I explained, showing him while I was talking, that someone had added a dictionary to the hard drive, and you could update it by adding new words. He did not seem overly impressed, but he watched carefully.

Some time later, while typing a document I found misspelled words that had not been corrected. When the computer gave me options, there appeared words that I had never seen on my computer—or in any dictionary—but ones I had helped my brother to correct. Calmly, I asked him to "Come here. Now!" I showed him the words and asked what might have happened. He explained that he had added the words so that they would not be misspelled. I almost had to agree it made sense.

There is a moral here. Stick by the rules until you've learned them.

- Rule #1: Follow the rules.
- Rule #2: Selur eht wollof.

Claim the Story

You have found a story. It may have come from an existing volume of stories or it may be one that you created. How do you prepare yourself to tell the story? Notice, I did not say, "How do you learn or memorize the story?" How do *you* prepare *yourself* for the story?

Here is an offering from my tradition. You will also find that it is shared by many cultures around the world. However, it is by no means the only tradition. You may find it all useful or portions of it useful. Be selective according to what works for you.

Absorb the story

In the beginning, do not give the story any more thought. Once you have selected the story, enjoy it. Immerse yourself in the story. One temptation is to try to learn the story. This is not the time to analyze its various aspects. Do not make an outline and concentrate on learning it. Just absorb the story.

Sit back and read the story, concentrating on nothing but the feel and sound of the story. Let the characters and words become familiar to you. Carry copies of the story with you. Place them throughout the house, or in your car. Read the story as often as you are able.

If it is helpful, type the story, or write it in longhand. Type the story again. Do not concentrate on any aspect of the story, just become familiar with it. Read the story out loud, feeling the flow of the words coming off of your tongue. Read with expression, but do not concentrate on characters or expressions. Do this over a period of weeks, even months if you are able. Just read. Absorb the story.

Record the story while you are reading it. Whenever you have a moment, play the story. Choose not to listen to the sound of your voice or your expression. Simply let the story play over you.

What you are doing is getting a feeling for the story as a whole. There will be time to break the story into segments and look at character, but this allows you to experience your story as a whole over and over. Stories have rhythms. There should be a rise and fall to the story. As you read it, type it, and listen to yourself read it, you will find that you subconsciously feel the story. You get a grasp of the whole story and also how *you* identify its rhythms.

Identify Areas of Personal Interest

Without concentrating on specific words or phrases, identify areas of personal interest in the story. At this point, do not ask for the input of others. Trust your instincts. As you tell the story, it is the things that excite you that you will be able to communicate best. Close your eyes as you listen to the story again. What captures your imagination?

Read the story again. Pay attention to those areas of interest. Begin to look at the story as a collection of key interest points. At this point, you should have a sense of the story as a whole; its rhythms and flow, and the things that excite you about the story.

Visualize the Story

Unless you are reciting a copyrighted text, put memorization on the back burner. There may be elements of your story that you may need or wish to memorize (Scripture, poetry, songs), but memorization can actually inhibit effective storytelling. Once you rely on memorization, you become dependent on it. Losing your place can be frightening, and memorization limits flexibility. Remember, storytelling is interacting with the audience. Interaction requires communication, and communication becomes difficult if you are locked into a script.

Among the Northern Plains tribes, events were recorded on winter-count robes. Such robes were called winter-count because the symbol(s) representing winter would tell the viewer the length of time that had passed since the robe was begun.

In the center of a buffalo robe, the maker would place a symbol representing a critical event in personal, family, or tribal life. It might be a symbol for birth, death, drought, good hunting, war, hail, a journey, or any other memorable experience. From that center, in spiraling line, the events would unwind. Others might pick up the robe after the death of its maker and continue the circle, providing information on a people that spanned many years. So universal were the symbols that even today we are able to begin at the middle and have a basic understanding of the events that impacted a person and her or his community.

In learning the long traditional stories of my Native people (some lasting many hours), I was taught to think of them as spirals. Each image gives way to another image until the story is complete. Every story is a succession of spiraling images. The role of the storyteller is to assemble the images, first in his or her own mind, and then to describe the images. The story unfolds as each image is revealed.

Do you remember flannelboards? In a time not so really long ago, most Sunday schools and public schools had large boards covered in flannel. As stories were told, cutout pictures of people, trees, rocks, and sheep were added to complete the scene. People actually traveled around the country with suitcases full of flannelboard materials! The children in my Sunday school class when I was growing up were always a bit confused as we received boxes of used Sunday school materials several years old. There were never enough flannelboard figures of the right kind, so our teachers were always saying, "Pretend this woman is Joseph," or "The shepherds were watching flocks of sheep, but we'll just have to let this camel stand in." You betcha!

Try to imagine each scene of your story as if it were a flannelboard. Picture it in your mind. If it is helpful for you, lay out separate pieces of paper or 4x6 cards to create an image-sheet for each scene. In whatever form is the most effective for you, note

- Background: Where did this scene take place?
- Characters: Who are the people, animals, or others who appear in the story?
- Events: What happens in the story?

When the image is complete, when the picture is finished, lay the paper down and step away from the scene. You are not after words. You are after images. If you have an image solidly in your mind, you will be able to share that image with others, even if you have not memorized a story. The images that you have selected are important, because they are what drew you to this story. You will not forget the images that you value.

As you continue to do this over time, you will discover that you will naturally begin to think in images. As you hear stories, you will recall them as images. You will be able to weave several small stories into a theme, each of them in your mind as an image. Choose what is best for you. You may prefer to think of stories in terms of slide shows or photo albums. It is the concept of images rather than memorization that is important.

Add the Senses

With the images in place, we have a good understanding of what we are able to see. Now ask, "What are we able to feel, taste, touch, or smell?" Do not think in terms of dialogue, but ask what the character(s) would experience. What does it feel like when the wind blows? What does the grass smell like? How would you describe these things for yourself?

There is a beautiful story attributed to the Lakota, with roots among Cheyenne oral literature. It is the story of *Jumping Mouse,* or *The Mouse Who Jumps.* I have heard this story all of my life, and it remains one of my favorites. There are several versions in print; most are not accurate to the originals (there are several). Since the story is part of oral tradition, it belongs to a people, and not to me. I do not choose to write it for that reason. It is not mine, and I respect the traditions of those storytellers who have gone before me.

In the story, a field mouse hears a roaring sound and despite discouragement from other mice, follows the sound to the banks of a great river. The sound leads him on a journey of discovery, where he is compelled to give away many of the things he values most. Ultimately he gives away his identity.

In the traditional version of this story, great emphasis is placed by the storyteller on what the mouse touches or is touched by. The storyteller emphasizes key words, which point to what is happening on a sensory level to the mouse. We are made to understand that when the mouse brushes up against a rock and the action ruffles its fur, providing that information to listeners is important. It is important because the mouse is experiencing something new, which alters its worldview. The touch is important, because once touched, the mouse is never the same again. While events and dialogue are important, what is most important is that how the mouse perceives the world is changing. (I read an Anglicized version of this great story. It had been reduced to fit on less than half a page. It was a synopsis of characters and events. The most remarkable elements of the story had been removed to save space.)

Before you can share a story with an audience, you must go beyond the words of the story to understand what sensations are taking place. By understanding them yourself, you are able to flesh out the story in a way that your audiences can experience.

Respond to the Story

Be yourself! As you experience both the visual and sensory images, what is your response to the story? Allow yourself to experience the whole story by the use of images and sensory information. How does that alter the story for you? The response that you feel will help establish your spirit as you tell this story.

Several colleges and universities offer undergraduate and advanced courses or degrees in oral literature or storytelling. I had been invited to sit on a panel of judges for a storytelling festival involving college-age students from across the United States. I am always hesitant about such competitions because they overlook the process of learning, and many people are discouraged from trying again.

In the preliminary rounds, several young people had told stories using a variety of styles. A name was called, and a young woman from Mississippi moved toward the stage. She was attractive and warm, greeting people with a thick Southern accent while we readied the paperwork. When everything had settled into place, she was introduced. Like a pitcher winding up for a curve ball, she lifted her arms, assumed a pose and began speaking. Gone was the warm Southern accent that made you feel at ease. Instead it was replaced with an artificial tone, designed to mimic other storytellers. Her gestures were practiced and choreographed. She would turn from side to side as she changed characters. When the story ended, her muscles relaxed, she assumed her own personality, smiled, and stepped to the side of the stage.

I try not to offer criticism but rather to offer praise. I try to lead students to think of alternatives that will give them some latitude of choice. I wrote several comments, and concluded with, "Were you comfortable with this style? How much of this is *you*?"

She did not make the final rounds of competition (never give up). During lunch the next day, she and her father joined me at my table. We sat and talked for an hour. I asked her to tell me about her family and where she grew up. She spoke of why she wanted to tell stories. Her warm voice resonated with laughter. I recognized the same style in her father. When it was time for me to go, I thanked them for sharing their stories with me (they hadn't realized they were telling stories). I told them that in that hour, they had pulled me into Mississippi and left me with a desire to hear more. As an afterthought, I added, "This is you!"

Four years later, in Asheville, North Carolina, I attended a storytelling event as part of a Southern Appalachian Arts festival. A young woman was introduced as a featured storyteller. In a rich southern accent, she told stories of being raised in the South and four generations of family living within one mile of each other. With the rest of the audience, I laughed, cried, and wished I were in Mississippi.

Look for Key Phrases

Key phrases can be several things. They can be beautifully crafted word combinations. They may be elements to trigger dialogue. In regard to visualization, they may be the words that trigger key action within the scene. Key phrases or key words are *your* selection of important elements to remember. They help *you*. They summarize an event or scene for *you*. They are tools that *you* devise to help you remember or to make the story more interesting for your audience.

Key phrases are not lengthy passages. They are points of references. Often, as I am preparing to speak, I will jot five or six words or word combinations onto a file card. At an event, there is seldom any time (no matter how well planned) to put your thoughts together at the last minute. As I have a second or two, I will look at the words and then put the card away. It is a reminder of key phrases that trigger memory.

Practice, Practice, Practice!

Practice doesn't make perfect, but it does create new habits. New habits, at least for me, do not take shape in a vacuum. They replace old habits. We do not tend to consider such a thing as the way we think to be a habit, but it is. Our pattern of doing things is determined by our upbringing and culture. It is also determined by what we have found successful, even on a subconscious level. It is the way we have always done it.

The way we have always done it can be changed, if there is a need to do so.

Some tribes selected leaders by consensus. A leader was one who had undertaken a leadership role in times of crisis. Among other tribes the chief was selected hereditarily, usually being approved by a woman's council or female members of the clan. An important quality of any chief was how he treated women and children. He also had to be able to inspire confidence among his people. The Cheyenne, particularly, valued smiling as a social skill. I once asked an older Northern Cheyenne friend how a person could develop smiling as a habit. His answer was simple and to the point. "Just start smiling," he said. "Pretty soon it sticks."

Shift From Words to Visuals

It is a difficult matter to make the shift from word-orientation to visual-orientation. Words are just as important as images. They are your tools to communication. But sometimes we are insecure about any form of public speaking without lots of printed words in front of us. The key is to trust your words, by trusting your process. That's a change of habit.

If you are a student in high school or college, there are two public speaking disciplines that will help you in storytelling. If you haven't been a student for many years, they will also help. One is dependent on ideas, and the other on memorized words. One will help you trust your own memory and ideas, and the other will help you present stories in a reading or recitative format.

- Extemporaneous speaking is usually included in forensics/public-speaking programs. Once you get past your initial fear of feeling unprepared, it can be a marvelous growing experience. As its name denotes, extemporaneous speaking limits the time you have to prepare before you speak. Usually forty minutes to an hour before an individual is to make a presentation, he or she is given a specific topic. Using books, periodicals, and other resources, the speaker prepares an eight- to ten-minute speech, with or without notes, around the theme. Hands sweating yet? What extemporaneous speaking teaches you is the ability to organize your thoughts quickly and summarize the topic. What you discover is that while you might not have a huge amount of specific information about a given topic, you are able to form an informed opinion. One of the best ways to open and conclude an extemporaneous speech is through the use of visual images.

  I was present at the national collegiate forensics finals several years ago. In most unusual fashion, the young man who placed first in extemporaneous speaking used a biblical comparison each round I heard him. He compared the iron curtain to the walls of Jericho. He compared utopian societies to the Garden of Eden. In short, from the back of his memory, he pulled stories that served as the foundation for his topic.

  I have heard great storytellers, those who are the most creative in friendly competitions of creating stories. A theme will be handed to them on the spot, with a few ingredients or characters. Without blinking, they will begin a narrative including all of the elements, to the delight of those listening. While it is a gift to be able to create stories on the spot, it is mostly discipline. Collective observations gained through the years, remembrance of pieces of story line and characters, and the ability to visualize all add to the moment.

- Interpretive reading is also an event in forensics competitions. Participants are encouraged to bring at least two selections from literature or poetry that illustrate a theme. They practice in advance and are allowed to use a copy of the text. Those who do the best memorize the text. Emphasis is placed on the relation of the selection to the theme, presentation, pronunciation, voicing, pacing, and so forth.

While I'm not certain that interpretive reading makes one a better storyteller, it does help develop many of the skills we use in storytelling. It also is effective for reading someone else's work. Since storytellers are often asked to read stories, it is great practice, and can be practiced alone.

Improvisational training can also be helpful to storytellers. Improv will ask you to create a scene (dramatic or humorous) around a topic given to you a moment before. As ominous as it sounds, most people improve rather rapidly. As a creative learning tool it has great value.

I once watched a mother of five who was also a junior high teacher tackle an improv class. By the third time, she was a pro. After receiving many compliments, she replied that having five children and teaching the seventh grade had prepared her for anything!

Many of the above forms of public performance are available at most schools. (Adults may also attend some classes at public schools. It is worth checking out.) Universities, junior colleges, amateur groups, community centers, and some churches have similar classes. If you have several people in your community, church, or group who have similar interests, consider asking someone familiar with these approaches to coach you. Being part of a small group with people you know can make the experience easier and much more fun. If professional coaches or teachers are not available, ask your school or college for students willing to help.

One observation: If you are able, whenever you do something for yourself that makes you a better communicator, share it with someone else as soon as you can. Consider children. What are barriers to adults may be prevented in children if they are given the opportunity. Storytelling starts in childhood.

Listening as Practice

One of the best ways to practice storytelling is to listen to storytelling. Every time you have a chance, listen. Most libraries have videos or recordings of storytellers. If you are listening to a recording, find a place to close your eyes. Remember putting your head down on the desk in elementary school? It's the same principle. It helps your focus!

As much as possible, watch storytellers. It helps you see what works physically. Be a sponge, but keep only what is effective for you.

Practicing on Your Own

Storytelling is public performance. That does not always mean large groups. It may mean your family, your church, or a public library. Part of your practicing needs to be performing in front of someone. If possible, create a group, say three people, who are interested in storytelling. Work through the process together. Go together to read to children at the library, daycare, or church. Next time choose to tell a story. Many urban schools need people to tell stories and read. There are many opportunities for practicing, beginning storytellers. The key is to get in front of *people.*

As much as storytelling practice needs to be public, it also needs to be private. Much of storytelling is self-nurture (not self-torture). You need time to yourself to absorb the story, reflect, think, say things out loud, and understand the story. As you become more comfortable being in front of audiences, much of your preparation of a story is spent when you are in the company of yourself.

The space you choose for practice is important. Find a spot that is comfortable for you. Find a place you enjoy being. You may have to work around the schedules of other people, but once you claim it, make it your own. It is important that you find a space where you will not be disturbed. Bring refreshments. Practice can be tough work.

Here's an odd suggestion. Many people find movement helpful to the thought process. Walking or pacing can be helpful. Sitting in a rocker and rocking will also help relax you and enable you to think more clearly. This is a learning process. Make it easy on yourself.

Visualizing Out Loud

We have talked about preparing yourself for the story. As you become familiar with the story, begin to tell it. This is not a presentation. This is visualizing out loud.

- *Tell yourself the story of the first picture.* You have identified the first scene. What do you want the audience to know? It may not be important for the audience to know everything that you do. Do you need to set the surroundings? If so, begin by describing the background, adding each image as necessary. Does a character enter at this point? Describe the character in as much or as little detail as you need (you will adapt this later). What events take place? Are there words (narrative or dialogue) or just movement? As you have prepared your picture, your visualization, tell yourself out loud what is taking place. What works for you? Don't worry about perfecting it just yet. You are building a house, and this is just the framing.

- *Try telling the story to yourself.* Move through each scene you have laid out. Are there things that need to be added? Are there things that need to be removed? Play with it until it makes sense. Then move on.

  As the story develops, you will feel more confident with it. Find a mirror and add it to your space. It needs to be large enough to show you from the waist up, and wide enough so that you don't have to stand in one spot. Start with scene one. Tell the scene. Watch your mannerisms and the way you use your eyes, smile, and hands. Don't try to do anything unnatural at this point. You are working on bringing yourself to the story. Just watch how you communicate. How would you like to communicate? Continue telling the story through each scene.

- *Keep the image-sheets that you have developed in front of you for as long as you need to.* (Review page 60 for more on image-sheets.) Read the story (if it is written) as often as you are able. Look at the key thoughts and phrases. You will know when you are comfortable.

  Try something different. Instead of the image-sheets, take a single note-card and create a story-card. No sentences, but a few simple words that will trigger memory for each scene. Leave a couple of spaces between each scene. Walking, pacing, or otherwise rhythmically moving, tell the story using the story-card. Still using the card, stand in front of the mirror and tell the story.

Many cultures around the world incorporate the use of something similar to the story-card. In Africa, Australia, and some parts of Asia, storytellers use a variety of storytelling sticks, with symbols representing images from the story. Do not be afraid to assemble things that will serve as visual reminders to you. You will need them less and less, but as we will see in the next section, many can serve as storytelling props.

As you practice, remember:

- Do not be on a timeline. You are learning new skills.
- Practice in a familiar and relaxed setting.
- Include easy, rhythmic movement, which helps you to relax and facilitates memory.
- Close your eyes and visualize each scene. Describe the scene.
- Think process. Grow in steps.
- Be accepting of yourself.
- Use the mirror as a reflection, not a judgment. Tell yourself the story in a way that pleases you.
- As you prepare for public storytelling, think about a group of people with like interests.
- Explore other forms of public performance as skill builders and confidence boosters.
- Try reading stories as an introduction to audiences.

Scary Story #3: The Haunted Autograph

Book signings have always been difficult for me. Culturally it conflicts with my traditional beliefs that you should avoid situations where you are putting yourself in front. Unfortunately, publishers do not see it quite that way. I have tried to make it a point to connect with as many people as possible, and though it takes longer, it has given me a purpose in what would otherwise be an awkward time.

On one occasion people had been waiting awhile for me to arrive. It wasn't that the book was that popular but that lunch was better, and they were trying to squeeze me in. After about twenty-five people had gone through the line, a young woman arrived with five books. I smiled and asked if I should sign them for someone in particular. She did not smile, and said yes, she would tell me what to write. She spelled a name for me, and said, "Write, 'To the best storyteller I have ever heard.'" I laughed; she didn't. I said, "I've never heard this person tell stories." She replied, at what I assumed was the upper register of her voice, "Look, just sign the books the way I tell you." So much for connecting, I thought. I signed all five books, being instructed to write, "To the best storyteller I have ever heard."

Six months down the road, I received a call at home. Someone I did not know was calling with a complaint. They had paid a storyteller on my recommendation and had a terrible experience. Since I did not know the storyteller, I simply said they must be mistaken. "But," the voice countered, "She sent us a copy of where you had written, 'To the best storyteller I have ever heard.'"

To date, I have had three such complaints. There are several morals to this story. Three of them involve my kicking myself. Even what appears to be harmless can be hurtful. It is better to say "no" and be credible. Unless you have heard another storyteller, don't vouch for that person's skill or character. Character is everything. Kick! Kick! Kick!

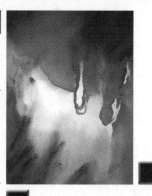

Part IV

Listeners and Hearers—Storysharing

How can one tell a story if no one listens? Storytelling is a relationship between the speaker and listener. At its best, it is not a "telling" but a sharing—storysharing. No matter the size of the audience, each person listening experiences the story in a personal way. Sharing story is human-to-human contact. Although the storyteller cannot determine how an individual may respond, the storyteller can do many things to both welcome and assist the listener.

Our home, as I was growing up, had frequent visitors. My mother, who is a wonderful cook, made meals a festival. We were not middle-class by any comparison, but in our home, there were candles for warmth, flowers for beauty, and food prepared and given with love. Ours was a home where people liked to come. Around our table, people were treated with respect, and they, in kind, were gracious guests.

One of the people we enjoyed the most was an old cowboy from Wyoming. He had been a bull-rider, and "between opportunities" had performed as a trick-roper. He always wore cowboy boots and a Resistol hat, with a big polished buckle. We called him "Mr. Art," which everyone else also did. When Dad would ask him to say grace, he would begin the prayer the same way he began all prayers, "Lord, this is Art."

Our friend had large, busted hands that matched his face. But, oh, they could make a rope sing! He called the rope "tangle-chord," and I never knew if that was its proper name or a nickname for when things didn't go quite right. He would fashion a small loop, a hondo, on one end and pull the straight end through it. He had small ropes and big ropes, all lying in easy coils. Sometimes, in the house, he would take a small rope and show us how to spin it, making perfect circles. But the thing that I remembered most was when the children all gathered around outside. He would spin a large rope, lifting it over his body and down again, standing in the middle. With his right hand he would take a smaller rope, place it between his teeth, and with his head making a gentle circle, spin the small rope with his mouth. On days when he felt particularly pleased with himself, he would spin the large rope and jump in and out of it while still spinning the small rope in his teeth.

He was a cowboy. He had rounded up herds in Montana and Wyoming. He had ridden in blizzards to take medicine to Native communities. His knees were so bowed you could put Idaho between them and still have room. He was the genuine article.

Mr. Art was a storyteller. He talked about bears and wolves. He told stories about cowboys that had never been bucked and broncs that had never been ridden. He told about heroes and villains, and he had known them all. For us, he was all of them.

More than anything else, our friend was like no one else. The hands were real. The face had been hard-won. The stories were real, told by one who had lived them. He was a real person, a human being.

It is the person I recall—sitting around my mother's table holding a teacup that didn't fit his hand, and laying a napkin on a bowlegged knee. It is the person I re-member best, spinning stories, like the ropes in his bag, uncoiling them and jumping in and out.

The story you share with others the most effectively will be the story that fits you. It may have been a hand-me-down, but it will have been tailored just for you. This is not to say that you may not tell a story that many others before you have told. It is simply to recognize that the elements of a story that attract you may be different than those that have attracted other storytellers. In addition the manner in which you tell a story will be distinct, and even though the story will be essentially the same, the vehi-cle through which the story is carried will be significantly different.

There are many intangibles that characterize an individual storyteller. All of the ingredients that shape your personality come into play as you tell a story. The accu-mulations of your life experiences, your values, your comfort with other people, your experience as a story-listener, and your life at this particular moment in time enter into your presentation of the story. As storytellers, we may borrow ideas from each other, but we may also tell the same story and identify unique aspects in the story. In the entire world there is no one else exactly like you.

Who are you? Do you have preferences for the type of stories you like to tell? Do you prefer to tell stories that are true? Do you prefer humorous stories to dramatic stories?

Do you prefer telling stories to adults rather than children? Do you tell stories in a physical way with audience involvement, or do you prefer a narrative style?

Who you are impacts not only the stories you choose to share but also the man-ner in which you tell them. And, although storytellers often excel at one or two types of story, we tend to tell publicly those stories that suit our style and comfort. It is not only acceptable but expected that we develop our own style of story and presentation.

What is important during the process of discovery is to explore a variety of stories and styles that may attract you and also to understand the basics of communication skills. By understanding the many options for success, we are able to make comfort-able choices that help us identify "who we are" as storytellers.

Certainly, the first choice that we make at this moment is in determining why we want to tell stories. This, like most of the choices that we will make, is not a "once and for all" choice but a choice for this moment. Do we wish to be better storytellers for our children or for a class that we may teach? Do we wish to tell stories more effectively in our public speaking? Do we wish to be storytellers as an avocation or as a vocation? What is it that we wish to achieve at this moment?

Most of the skills that we will learn as storytellers will have value in other applications. Like all skills, most are best learned over a period of time, as you alter old habits and acquire new ones. Think of storytelling skills as those that you acquire over a lifetime, and resist the temptation to expect immediate results. Enjoy the process, and love what you do.

Key Elements of Public Speaking

Several years ago, a young man actively involved in public speaking was describing what he called "the day-after experience." It involved stiffness in the joints of his legs, a hoarse voice, and extreme fatigue. While he was speaking, he further experienced the sensation of not being able to get enough air and having air run out in the middle of sentences. Though it was obvious that a fair number of these physical symptoms came from nervous tension, some seemed to suggest lack of training in basic skills.

I had the opportunity to listen to him speak that evening. He was well informed and interesting. His stories were rich and colorful. He was also rigid. With knees locked, he stood in one spot. His hands moved comfortably, but his shoulders were stooped. There was never a moment when he varied his voice. From beginning to end he maintained the same intensity. The ingredients were there for an interesting speaker. Few would have been distracted by his bad habits. Unfortunately, his body, and his spirit, paid a price for not learning the basics.

As you have prepared for public speaking, you will have undoubtedly acquired a great many new skills to help you in the process. There are some elements of storytelling that are unique to the performing arts rather than to most public speaking. They have to do with maintaining your voice, physical endurance, projection, and ease of presentation. Some relate specifically to how your audience perceives you.

Posture

Good posture will increase your ability to project your voice (be heard), breathe, move comfortably, endure long periods of standing, and reduce tension. All that from posture!

In most cases, your feet should be shoulder-width apart, and your knees flexible (not locked). This will prevent you from falling but also prevent dizziness due to tension. What you are after is good blood flow (oxygen), balance, and comfort. You remember the movement that we practiced as we learned our story? A good stance also contributes to good memory.

Beginning with arms at your sides, lift them straight above your head until they are pointing toward the sky. Slowly lower your arms. Imagine that there is a string from the back of your head, lifting straight upward. Pretend that there is also a string from the middle of your chest, lifting straight upward. Your chest should be lifted up, and the back of your head lifted up. If the back of your head is lifted correctly, your chin will be in proper placement. Breathe in through your nose slowly, and exhale through your mouth slowly. Stand quietly for a moment and just breathe. Feel the placement of your feet, knees, chest, and head. This is home base. This is where you come back to. As often as possible throughout the day, use this simple exercise to determine correct posture.

Breathing

If you are a singer or an actor, you are familiar with the phrase "speak or sing from your diaphragm." Most all of us are never really sure where the diaphragm is located. We have an idea that it has to do with muscles located in or near the abdomen, but other than that, we haven't a clue how to speak from the diaphragm. Here are some elements:

The diaphragm is not the front of your stomach. The diaphragm is most accurately referred to as the diaphragm sheath, a series of muscles running internally across the body, separating the lungs and heart from the intestines and other organs. As you inhale and your lungs expand, they force the diaphragm to bend downward, giving the lungs more room. As you expend air, the diaphragm bends upward, forcing air out of the lungs.

All of this happens as a matter of course every minute of every day, all of your life.

What makes singing or speaking different? As you speak or sing, air passing over the vocal chords, or vocal folds, causes them to vibrate, creating sound. The purest sound in singing is created with the smallest amount of air. How can you control air? You control air by manipulating the expansion or contraction of the diaphragm, breathing in or expelling air through the lungs. Learning to control breathing allows you a variety of options.

When you breathe correctly, your chest should neither rise nor fall. Instead, your chest should remain upright in a normal position. There are two different schools of thought on what should happen next. In one school, it is believed that the abdominal area should extend outward, in the same manner as an infant lying on its back expands its muscles before a cry. You can test this form of breathing by lying on your back. As you breath in, extend your abdominal muscles outward. As you exhale, consciously pull your abdominal muscles inward and upward, expelling air from the lungs through your mouth. Do it again. Breathe in through your nose, expanding your abdominal muscles. Exhale slowly through your mouth, pulling the abdominal muscles inward and upward.

The second school of thought is related more to musical theater, belt/pop, pop, rock, and even hip-hop music. Instead of expanding the abdominal muscles, you still maintain your posture, and the rib cage is expanded from side to side rather than outward. This allows for a brighter, more staccato sound in the upper register. It is also useful in storytelling or theater for making loud or percussive sounds without straining the vocal chords. Forcing movement of the diaphragm quickly controls the flow of air. Save this technique for advanced work in voice control.

With proper posture and breathing, you can speak longer, be heard better, and stand in front of crowds without causing yourself pain or injuring your voice. Posture and breathing are not everything, but they are the foundations upon which you can build many other more easily acquired skills.

Projection

As a storyteller, you will most often have access to a microphone. A microphone is a great tool for picking up the subtleties of the voice. However, before you become comfortable with a microphone, prepare for the inevitable: The microphone does not work, or you are in an arena that does not allow for microphones.

Projection is the art of being heard without damaging your voice. With proper projection, you will utilize breath control, your vocal instrument, and sound placement to be heard well, while still producing a variety of sounds. Long before sound amplification, orators, preachers, actors, and storytellers learned the skills that made their voices carry with expression over large audiences in all types of settings. Here are some things we have learned over the centuries:

- Low breathy sounds cannot be heard well over distance. Higher sounds carry farther.
- Use of the diaphragm (controlling the flow of air) while speaking carries the sound farther.

In singing, we use the phrase "head tone" to refer to resonating sounds through the bones, sinuses, and mouth. Head tones carry a greater distance than do sounds produced only in the throat. Head tones may have a marginal nasal sound to them, such as in folk, bluegrass, traditional country, Middle Eastern, and other forms of ethnic music. In nations where Islam is the predominant religion, the call to prayer is sung out over the city, the head tone of the singer carrying the call over long distances.

As storytellers, we often use both the diaphragm and the head tone to project our voices. By controlling the flow of air, and the placement of the sound, we preserve our voices and enable others to hear.

Facial Expressions

Remember standing in front of the mirror? As awkward as that experience can be, few of us perceive ourselves as others perceive us. Feedback from others is important, but feedback from *you,* at least in the area of facial expression, should come first. While most of us do not like the sound of our own voices, most of us have a good idea of how we would like to appear in the process of storytelling. Appearance is not necessarily an acquiring of expressions and mannerisms that are not your own, but it is maximizing the unique characteristics that others see as "you."

Facial expressions may be reflecting what you are saying and what is happening within the story. If your story is upbeat and joyful, you probably do not want to appear frightened or angry. If your story is funny, your facial expressions can help pull audience participants into the mood of the story. However, there are some exceptions that you may encounter where your facial expressions should not reflect the mood of the story.

Not all cultures associate direct eye contact with honesty. In some instances other cultures believe prolonged eye contact does not allow people the privacy of their true feelings. Intruding into areas of privacy can be a social error. Storytelling is an exception to that rule in most cultures. It is an exception unless your audience is very small. Because you are not engaging one person, but several, as a storyteller, you have the option of eye contact without selecting one person in particular. Facial expression becomes a tool of communication for multiple participants rather than an intimate conversation.

An individual sitting in an audience may not wish to be singled out, but he or she may wish to experience the story through you, the storyteller. There is also a desire for you to guide each person into understanding how she or he should respond. You do that with your facial expressions. To a large degree, how you feel about a given story is how you should convey your emotions. You, the storyteller, grant permission for the audience participants to experience the emotion by experiencing it yourself.

One of the most difficult stories I share with audiences has as its theme the death and loss of Native communities during times of cruelty and persecution. The events of the true story are painful and awkward. The difficulty is in offering the story and encouraging people to "hear" what is being said. The natural inclination in listening to such stories is to put up a series of barriers for self-protection. We listen to the story, but we shut out the human response to empathize with those in the story.

What is the theme of the story? The events are death, loss, enslavement, cruelty, and separation. But the theme is really forgiveness. The theme is survival and beyond. It is learning to love those who hurt you, so that you do not choose to hurt them in return. I knew these people. Many were family members. Theirs was an experience of reconciliation initiated by those who themselves had been the targets of abuse. How would they have conveyed the story? What would they have wished for the audience to feel? I remember how their faces looked when they told me the story. I see those faces still.

When they spoke about a massacre where many of their families had been killed, they wept, but there was no anger or animosity. When they spoke about unkindness and abuse, they told the truth, but their faces were gentle. When they spoke about forgiveness, they smiled, leaned forward, and nodded their heads. They were inviting me into understanding the choices and why they were made.

There are times as storytellers when the facial expressions are honest, but are contrary to the events of the story. It is okay to demonstrate love while describing hate. It is a good thing to show forgiveness when talking about injustice. When we make those choices, we communicate with those who listen that events do not always determine response, and we invite them to do the same. Our personal characters and the intent of the story are what guide us. There is a difference between being entertaining and choosing to be transparent. At the moment of our transparency, we become credible.

Someone in the audience will hear the story, and know that he or she is not alone.

Modulating Voice and Speed

If variety is the spice of life (sometimes), then vocal modulation is the spice of a story. Imagine listening to someone speak for an hour at the same intensity, speed, and pitch. It has the same effect as hearing background noise. After a while, the words and sound run together and form a type of white noise.

Have you ever spoken to a group of noisy children? What happens when you lower your voice almost to a whisper and begin to speak to just a few? Before long a few more strain to hear, followed by others, until the group of children has pulled close, trying to listen. Modulating your voice creates interest.

Volume is not the only tool of modulation. Intensity and speed are great variables. Dialogues and narratives can both be made more interesting by speeding up the flow of words, as well as by changing the intensity of your voice and facial expressions.

Particularly in dialogue, but also for effect, alternating the pitch of your voice can denote a change in character or a change in mood. Lowering (deepening) the voice may be a signal of one character, and raising (to make higher) the voice may be a signal of another character. Raising the pitch is also a universal sign of excitement, and lowering the voice a signal of secrecy. Lowering the voice and increasing the speed denotes both secrecy and excitement. If you wish to build in intensity and excitement, begin with a low voice, and gradually increase both the pitch and speed.

Silence

Silence creates drama. In the middle of a flow of words, silence becomes the exception and commands our attention. In reality every listener to a story perceives the story differently. That is one of the great values of storytelling. To each listener, the story takes on a variety of messages. Silence allows the listener a wide range of possibilities. It is the unspoken story within a story. It is the place of the ultimate imagination. Silence is the unknown.

I once heard a great salesman comment, "Never be afraid of silence. Rather, be afraid that you will say too much, and take your client too far."

Silence can be used to create intensity or drama. It can be followed by a change in pitch or speed. Silence can be used to switch scenes or characters, or simply to add variety. Silence is one of the best friends of a storyteller.

Repetition, Repetition, Repetition

At the risk of repeating myself, repeat yourself, often. Repetition is one of the fastest ways to commit something to memory. In making phrases familiar, the storyteller helps the listener recall elements of the story.

In Nigeria, I attended a large church. Several thousand people crowded into a large, wooden structure. The mostly Muslim Nigerian Army would occasionally walk through the church carrying Israeli-made Uzi rifles.

Looking around the congregation was like looking over a vast plain of color. Bright, vivid cottons in pinks, blues, oranges, purples, reds, yellows, greens, and bright whites vied for attention. I have never seen more beautiful colors before or since. Worship was not only celebration but also a quickening of the senses. One felt more alive, like a late-summer garden, surprised by a cool rain.

There were no songbooks. Singing was accomplished by lifting your head, smiling at everyone around you, and distributing joy. The harmonies flowed easily and richly, like the cottons. You could hear the color of the notes.

Prayer was like a spoken song. Everywhere, people would be praying out loud, the sounds of human voices mingling with one another, thickening the air. It seemed to go on for hours. When it wavered, someone would stir it into action again, the prayers winding around us in circular fashion. When it was time to stop, the pastor stood up and rang a large bell. The prayer-song softened. The bell was rung again, and the crowd stood quiet catching their breath.

The pastor was a large man, an imposing figure even at the distance of the platform. He greeted his flock, holding his hands palms open, facing the crowd as if to sense their warmth. "Jesus knows your name," he said, firmly and quietly. The crowd responded with deep throaty sounds. "Jesus knows your name," he said again, louder and joyfully. "Say it to each other," he directed. The colors moved, like flowers in the wind, as people said the words to as many as they could reach. "Say it to the soldiers," the pastor encouraged. People turned toward the soldiers standing in a few entrances, and said, "Jesus knows your name." Most of the soldiers left.

"Say it to your soul. Say, 'Soul, Jesus knows my name.'" The crowd spoke to themselves. Around the vast wooden structure, people were celebrating the God who knew their names.

As the pastor spoke, his voice rising and falling in deep and warm cadence, the phrase was repeated over and over. Time and again, he would ask us to repeat his words. More times he would say them to us, until we were as certain as we were of the warm sun and heavy air that Jesus knew our names.

We dispersed after the service, lingering for an hour or so to greet old friends and make new ones. The colors of cotton drifted away like petals on an August wind—each of us carrying an unwritten song that could not be forgotten, "Jesus knows my name."

Repetition is a tool to aid memory. The more we say something, read something, sing something, pray something, or write something, the more we will remember it. The more we involve others in the repetition, the more easily we will have assisted them in committing something to memory.

Repetition in story can take a variety of forms. It may be a line like "Not by the hair of my chinny-chin-chin." It may be a name, a theme, or a small song. Repetition may also be a movement or a gesture that implies much more. It may also be a facial expression that the audience will come to anticipate. We repeat to remember or cause others to remember.

Defining Characters

I am always reminded of the one-man bands of the last century. A person clad in trumpets, cymbals, drums, harmonicas, and an occasional concertina would stand on a street corner and play music. If the music was not too painful, passersby would toss a few coins in the hat, and the one-man band could eat that day. It is a little bit like a story with too many characters. There are only so many ways that one can tweet, plunk, boom, twitter, and trill.

Most storytellers can acquire simple skills for differentiating characters. What is important is that your audience has the ability to distinguish between characters in your story. One tool is modulating your voice. It is a simple matter to lower your vocal register for one character, or raise it for another. One can add nasal tones or breathy tones. One character may even speak slower or faster, with greater or less deliberateness. You need not be an accomplished mimic to be a good storyteller. You do, however, need to be consistent. Unless the change is part of the plot, your character's voice should remain constant throughout the story.

Another tool is body positioning or gestures. In simple dialogue, a storyteller may turn toward the right for one character, and turn slightly to the left for another. If a character has certain physical characteristics, you may illustrate them with your body position or the use of your hands. If the character has large antlers, you may place your hands over your head to illustrate antlers. If the character has a cavalier attitude, you may cross your feet (for a moment) and pretend to lean. If the character has a distinctive walk, you may move about in that fashion while the character is speaking.

Body position is an excellent tool combined with silence. If you wish to show a distinctive character in thought, assume your posture and be quiet. If you wish to show movement without words, move, but stay in character. One can actually show conflict or quiet between two or more characters by switching from one position to another without saying anything. Body position combined with facial expression can be an element of delight in story. Be inventive, but be consistent.

Adapting to Your Audience

Not all stories are appropriate for all settings. How do we determine what is appropriate for a given audience? Here are some questions to ask yourself or the individual or organization extending an invitation:

- What is the average age of the audience?
- Will the key elements of the story be understandable for everyone?
- Are there issues affecting or influencing this event or audience?
- Are there elements of the story that may be sensitive areas for this group?
- Why, specifically, were you asked to be present at this event?
- What obstacles do you anticipate may be present among audience attitudes?
- What is the racial-ethnic diversity of the audience?
- Are there common beliefs among most members of the audience?
- What time of day will you be on the program?
- Who or what will precede you on the program?
- What are the expectations of the group?
- What are the physical surroundings of the event?
- What is the time limit of your presentation?

All of these questions help you to evaluate the situation into which you have been invited to share stories. Some are elemental.

The Importance of Age Appropriateness

The age of the audience will affect almost everything that you do. Young children may enjoy the act of storytelling, but they may not understand the subtleties and nuances of a story intended for adults. Their attention spans are much shorter than those of adults. Children tend to take literally many things that are said and may not grasp metaphors within the story. Especially young children are not able to separate characters in a story from reality and tend to envision them as part of their everyday world. Simple themes work best, particularly if they are relevant to the world of the child. Conflicts need to be resolved. Children often need to see the story as a whole with a definite conclusion. If children are a large focus of the gathering, be prepared to be shorter in length, involve more animation, and select stories appropriate to their age and experience. If you are uncertain about what is age appropriate for a child, consult with teachers, counselors, Christian educators, or anyone trained specifically in working with children.

A good rule of thumb in preparing for any event is to ask who will be the target audience. If the target audience is largely adults, some of whom may bring their families, be prepared with stories aimed at adults, but with a story or two just for children. If families are the focus, aim the majority of your stories at the broadest number of people, but keep in mind that children may be the audience you need to connect with the most. Any family venue that does not appeal to children will not be effective for the family.

Most storytellers will agree that while youth call forth some unique considerations, the youth audience is not as difficult as one might suspect. They are a challenge in that their attention often must be earned and not just expected. However, they are a wonderful audience for understanding metaphors, conflict, dilemma, and complex subjects. They respond naturally to humor. In my experience, youth resist manipulation, but they respond to honesty, integrity, and credibility. If you are telling more than one story be prepared to use a variety of styles.

Why Are You Here?

It is important to know why you have been invited—not only why you are invited as a storyteller, but also why *you* particularly. This question is not necessarily easily asked. Sometimes this information is shared when the invitation is given. A good suggestion might be asking, "Are there specific things that you would like to see accomplished?" Sometimes your testimony, or personal story, may have significance to the event. Perhaps someone has heard you tell a specific story that has relevance to the moment. It is important to understand why you are being asked and to decide if you are comfortable with that expectation. If you are not comfortable with the expectations of the event, simply say, "Thank you for thinking of me. I may not be the best person to help you achieve your goals. Might I suggest _____?"

As a person of Native heritage, I weigh some invitations carefully. Is there an expectation that all of my stories will be Native-related stories? Am I being invited as a Native person or as a storyteller who is also Native? Are there expectations that I will wear tribal attire? As uncomfortable as it is, these are questions that I sometimes ask to prevent misunderstandings. Wherever you are from, whatever culture is yours, be comfortable with why you have been asked. It need not be a major concern, except where you feel expectations may be different from reality. An African American may choose to tell a story about a bonsai tree. A Southern woman may wish to share a story about winter in the subarctic. Diversity is not always an issue of skin color. Diversity is about experience and interest.

Know Your Audience

Knowing who is represented in your audience enables you to speak directly to them in a more effective way.

Recently, I had the opportunity to speak to a group of male and female prisoners in a minimum-security facility. Men and women were both invited to attend but sat on separate sides of the large room. I wasn't allowed to shake hands or have direct contact with them. In truth, many were there because they had nowhere else to go. The facility counselor explained to me that most were incarcerated due to substance abuse and the resultant petty crimes. When sober, they were caring, creative people. When under the influence of drugs or alcohol, they were very different.

When I was introduced, I stood for a moment looking over each face, not wanting to begin with a practiced line. I had extended-family members who had been incarcerated for long periods of time. I wanted to bring some joy, laughter, but also encouragement. I knew that perhaps many months later, when dialogue had slipped from memory, a story might come back to mind. I remembered, and believed, from my tradition that stories are living things. I believed, especially in that moment, that when a story is heard, and actualized, it has the potential to alter behavior. What could I say?

My brother, Rick, had hidden a small dreamcatcher in my suitcase. I had absentmindedly picked it up and put it in my coat pocket. Carefully I pulled it out. I remembered a phrase that I had heard as a child. The words, "I depend on you for strength," came to mind as I said them. I talked about the dreamcatcher, a collection of knots in the shape of a spider web, and how each knot depended upon the other for existence. I talked about how the dreamcatcher became unraveled if even one knot was broken. When the story was complete, I remembered how the story had ended when I first heard it. I repeated the words, "We are all related. Which knot can we do without? I depend on you for strength."

Sometimes there has been a death in a community. Sometimes a natural disaster or financial crises have devastated a community. Sometimes folks just need a good laugh. Some groups need something that will help them build a sense of community. Others wish to be spiritually encouraged. As you gather a series of stories that are meaningful to you, you will have greater ability to speak to a variety of situations. Understanding who is seated in front of you will offer you and your audience more opportunities for connection.

What Is the Nature of the Event?

There are some key questions to ask as you prepare for an event. Many times not all of the information is available at the time you are asked to attend. One of the best ways to avoid embarrassing situations or misunderstandings is to make sure that everyone is operating with the same information.

As silly as it may seem, it is important to know what time of day you are to tell stories. It is good to show up on time, but it is also good to know how the audience may be feeling when you are presenting. An early-morning presentation brings a mixture of early-risers and those-who-have-to-be-there-but-aren't-awake-yet. Midmorning to late morning is a time when most people are alert. After lunch and midafternoon are sleepy times. Early evening hours are often the best for stories, which is probably why in most traditional cultures evening is when stories are told. If you are asked what time you prefer (which is not very often) suggest late morning or early evening.

If you are given a specific time, though, be aware of how those in the audience might be experiencing the normal bodily flows during a day, and adjust your presentation accordingly.

Many people are unaware of the process of storytelling. Often people who have heard you tell a particular story will ask, "We would like for you to tell the _____ story. Can you do that in ten minutes?" If you are comfortable in doing so without compromising the story, feel free to agree. If the time limit is too short to do the story justice, you need to express that to your host well in advance. Sometimes trying to fit into an unrealistic time frame significantly minimizes the effectiveness of a given story. Both you and your host will be disappointed. When you are invited, make certain that the time allotted to you is sufficient, but not excessive. Many times that element is easily adjusted.

Knowing who or what will precede you on a program may help you determine how you begin. If you are to follow a business session, or a somber moment, know that you will have to work extra hard to pull your audience into the story. If you are following an upbeat musical presentation, it may take awhile for the audience to emotionally "come down" to settle into a storytelling experience. You may also want to ask if someone will be introducing you. Sometimes an introduction can make for a smooth transition. If there is an expectation that you will introduce yourself, think about ways to do that to fit a number of situations. That in itself is storytelling and can be a wonderful transition into your presentation.

Where Is the Event to Be Held?

As your experience in storytelling broadens, you will gain a feeling for different types of places. As much as possible, spend some time in the room or auditorium before the crowd arrives. Walk up the aisles and sit in some of the seats. Look at the platform or stage. Try to envision what the audience might see. Stand where you will be speaking. Look around to see all of the areas where the audience will sit.

Most events are accommodating. Storytelling is best shared when there is nothing between you and the people with whom you are sharing. If there is no space prepared other than a podium or pulpit, that will be okay. If you have an option, ask for a hand-held microphone or a lavaliere (clip-on). Know in advance who the sound engineer is going to be so that all arrangements are made. When you open your mouth to speak, you want every word to be heard. Sometimes that takes a little preparation.

Some of the best storytelling is done is small areas without the use of sound systems. These are usually intimate settings where you are closer to the audience. If you have input into how the space is arranged, here are some thoughts:

- Circles are wonderful for conversation, but they always exclude a portion of the people from seeing your face if you are in the center.
- Semi-circular seating is wonderful for creating a sense of community. The simple act of curving the ends of rows gives a feeling of inclusiveness and "drawing together."
- For children and those who are able to sit on the floor, having a special space for storytelling allows a feeling of comfortable warmth. Children especially

respond to a change of space in which they recognize a different set of actions and behavior. It helps to make a transition from one activity to another.

- It is important for you as the storyteller to be seen. Facial expression and body language are important visuals for those who are listening. If the audience is sitting on the floor, you have the option of using a chair. Remember to be close enough, so that your audience does not have to lean back to see you!
- Sometimes a medium-height stool is a good tool for any venue. It allows you to move from standing to moderate sitting with little effort. It offers a change of pace to the audience, and can serve a variety of purposes as a prop or a place to rest storytelling tools.
- Where will you be sitting prior to storytelling?
- What is appropriate attire for that setting?

The little things matter. The more at ease you are with everything else around you, the more you can focus on communicating with the people in front of you.

Being Sensitive

Understanding your audience involves doing your homework. If your audience shares common beliefs, know what they are and be sensitive to them. It is always best, unless asked to do otherwise, to find areas of commonality and to avoid divisive issues. You are present as a guest, and that comes with some responsibility. Here are some thoughts:

- *Find common ground.* Unless directed otherwise, make sure that your story or stories reflect the values of your audience. An exception might be the occasion in which you have been invited to share stories with a different point of view.
- *Be understanding.* If you are part of a worship service in a tradition other than your own, ask lots of questions so that you and the congregation are comfortable. When in doubt, always ask first. For example, gender-specific language in reference to God may be normal in some traditions, but it may be out of place in others. Know what matters and what doesn't.
- *Be an encourager.* Avoid remarks that may be construed as criticism of a group or belief system.
- *Be aware that your influence does not begin and end on the stage.* Your integrity, particularly as it relates to the values in the stories you share, is demonstrated by how you live and share at all times. In Christian tradition, we call this "living your faith." In Native traditions we do not tell stories that we do not embody in our choices.

A few years ago, I was asked to be present at a large meeting in the Midwest. While there, I met an acquaintance whom I admire greatly. Several times during my stay, I had the opportunity to see this wonderful individual, most often when surrounded by several other people. My acquaintance is from a related tribe. His language, Dakota, and mine, Lakota, are similar, but with some dialect differences.

Each time I would see him, although there were others waiting to speak to me, he would approach me and begin speaking in Dakota, completely ignoring the others around us. I would answer him in English. On the third time, both of us were embarrassed, but he was persistent.

Through my eyes, there were several things inappropriate about the situation. People were waiting to speak to me, and we could have arranged another time to visit by simply exchanging information in a note. Pushing in front of other folks diminished their importance and my responsibility to honor their presence. Speaking in a dialect that I did not fully understand, but no one else understood at all, also isolated us from the folks gathered around. In a public setting, one should not choose to communicate in a manner that excludes others.

Your "story" is being told the moment you walk through the door, until you leave.

I have a close friend who is a Christian musician. In a hurry to get to a concert on time, she rushed through a stop sign and pulled in front of a person waiting in line to get gas. When the person objected, she brushed the person off, filled her tank, and headed down the road.

As the concert began, and she was introduced, she walked across the platform and looked down into the eyes of the person she had brushed off at the gas station. She never forgot that moment.

Your "story" is being told every minute of every day. Be conscious of those around you and responsible toward them.

Audience Involvement

Interactive storytelling involves the audience in an active way during the telling of the story. The tools are often simple. You may teach the audience a word, phrase, or even a simple song, which they will speak or sing when they receive a cue from you, the storyteller. The use of repetition, an enormously valuable tool, takes on a new form by having the audience repeat certain portions of the story along with the storyteller.

Other forms of audience involvement may include asking audience members to represent key characters, offering them a piece of costume, a prop, or some distinguishing element. They can initiate a response at appropriate cues from you. For example, audience members may represent several key characters. You have prepared the audience in advance to respond to an exaggerated introduction of each character throughout the story. They will repeat the introduction, and the character will only respond to the next sentence. You, the storyteller, might say during the story, "And the knight . . ." in a loud voice. The audience will shout back, "And the knight . . ." You would complete the action by saying, ". . . skipped around the castle." Whereupon the audience member playing the role of the knight would skip around, and then wait for the next clue.

Other forms of audience involvement may include sound effects taught before the story begins. Light rain can be the sound made by rubbing the hands together. A medium rain can be made by the sound of an audience all clicking their fingers. Heavy rain may be imitated by the slapping of the hands on the thighs, and a thunderstorm by the stomping of feet on the floor.

There is an infinite variety of ways in which to involve the audience as part of the storytelling process. The key is preparation and timing. The audience needs to be clear as to what is expected of them, when they are expected to participate, and when to quit. That can be accomplished by explaining the process before the story begins and practicing with the audience. Expect that things will not go perfectly. That is part of the fun! Spontaneous things can and will occur, which will delight the audience even further. As a storyteller, you must be prepared for the unexpected, roll with the flow, and be able to bring the audience back.

Butterflies and Bats: Being Scared

Everyone gets stage fright. Well, not everyone, but a lot of us. It is a healthy, normal experience. Fortunately, as a storyteller you have the advantage of polishing a performance over several years. It is always the first couple of times that you feel uncertain. As you become familiar with yourself and your story, there are fewer unexpected things to fear.

I have a clergy friend who every so often has a time for sermon requests. Her congregation loves the chance to request their favorite sermon, but it also gives my friend an opportunity to revisit some excellent messages. As she puts it so well, "It's a shame to use a good sermon only once!" As a storyteller, you will have the opportunity to refine stories each time you present them. That will help ease anxiety.

You depend on your voice. Never stress your voice unnecessarily. One temptation, particularly if you are nervous, is to clear your throat. Be careful. Clearing your throat has the same effect as slapping your vocal chords together. Instead, swallow or drink something warm. Protect your voice. Never use sprays or cough drops that deaden the feeling in your throat. You may not be aware if you have gone too far.

Recognize that as you progress into a story, you will begin to relax. The most difficult part is simply getting started. Close your eyes and imagine yourself telling the story flawlessly. Imagine every gesture, every movement. You have practiced and prepared. Trust yourself.

Breathing is important to relaxation. Breathe in deeply through your nose, hold for a few seconds, and exhale slowly through your mouth. Tension can inhibit blood flow. Lack of blood flow prevents oxygen from getting through your body. Breathe.

Remember posture? Raise your arms above your head, aligning your spine. Imagine the strings at the back of your head and the middle of your chest. Lower your arms and breathe comfortably.

Bend over from the waist, letting your arms dangle in front of you. Hold the position as long as you are comfortable. Stand up slowly. You will notice that the flow of blood to your upper body has made your voice warmer and more relaxed. Breathe slowly for a while. Bend over again.

Pray. You have prayed while you were searching for a story. You have asked for assistance while learning the work. You have asked God to help you be yourself and do your best. Give the moment of the story to God. For this moment in time, whether you are in a church, a library, a public park, or your living room, you are engaged in a sacred act. You are a storyteller.

Pragmatics: Telling the Story

The moment has arrived. The audience has gathered or is gathering, and it is nearly time to begin. There is a wealth of feelings inside as you are completing last-minute arrangements. How you prepare yourself in these last moments is different for each storyteller. Sometimes there has been a place prepared for you to spend a few minutes alone. Many times folks are saying hello and reviewing the program with you. In a church or library setting, you may be busy setting up chairs or making last-minute adjustments. The important thing is, whenever and however you do it, make time for yourself. Preparing your spirit will be your greatest gift to those who will listen to your stories.

There are so many terms used for the process of preparing for a public performance. Depending on your culture and nationality, these terms may not be so familiar to you. Often the word *centering* is used for the process of excluding the busy-ness of the world around us and focusing on relaxation, prayer, or any other personal element.

Visualization has many applications, but in this process it refers to imagining yourself telling the story in just the way that you would like. Olympic athletes use visualization to imagine themselves completing a performance flawlessly. With that clearly in mind, they are able to initiate an event with the feeling of just having executed a successful program. As you tell a story several times, you will discover that you do not always need as much pre-program preparation specifically related to the story. What may be more relevant is preparing yourself for engaging the people who will share the story with you.

Attitude Is Everything

While in many ways storytelling is an art form, and you are to be appreciated as an artist, the best storytelling is genuine communication, not performance. The opportunity to share story is a gift, an opportunity that many people will never have. It is not to be approached arrogantly, but rather with humility and, in many ways, with a sense of purpose. You have been invited to influence people through one of the most effective means possible. How you approach that opportunity says a great deal about who you are. Here are some reminders:

- *Choose a story that you believe in.* Telling a story that doesn't fit your values and beliefs is a little like trying to sell a product you mistrust. If you believe in the story, every telling can be a fresh experience. If you believe in the story, those who watch and listen will be able to tell it in your eyes and mannerisms. If you are asking them to experience something on an emotional level, they will be more willing to do that if you are experiencing the story on an emotional level.
- *Reduce the story to the elements that are most important to you.* Unless you are telling a copyrighted work, not all elements of a given story need to be shared at one time. Identifying what is most important also helps you isolate what is most meaningful to you.
- *Wrap yourself in the story.* Become the story. As you infuse the story with yourself and try to give yourself to others through the story, you will discover that what becomes most important is the sharing of the story, not the concept of performance.
- *Be yourself.* You will be able to communicate the essence of the story best when it comes from your heart and voice. Allow people to see the person that you are. No one else can tell a story exactly like you.

- *Prepare yourself for the story.* Generations of people have viewed storytellers as culture bearers. While the story need not be lengthy or serious in nature, be true to the story, your culture, faith, and tradition. Leave the other concerns behind you and for whatever time it takes, become the story.
- *Be confident.* Remember the Cheyenne chiefs who learned to smile? Sometimes altering your behavior affects how you feel. Remember how you imagined yourself telling this story in the manner you felt was most effective? Tell it that way. Be confident. Be confident that those listening need the words to this story. Be confident that you are the person best suited for this moment to tell this story. Be confident that storytelling is a shared experience between teller and listeners. You are the sharer of story. Wrap the story around you and step out!

Connecting With the Audience

Every person you meet is different. Every person in the audience will hear your story in a different way. Most will find different areas of value in the same story. Your job is to connect with them. Oddly enough, it is not your job to identify those who may not especially like your story, or even those who enjoy it thoroughly. Your job is to connect with the broader audience; the folks in the middle; those who may be neither particularly negative or particularly enthusiastic. Talk to them. Pull them into the story so that they can experience it, glean from it, and take it home.

Love your audience. Let me say it again. Love your audience. Love the very distinct faces in the crowd. Love the people who have worked all day, rushed home to supper, and come out on an evening when they already have too much to do. Love the children who are anxious to listen to a story. Love the people in front of you. If you do nothing else well, do this; they will know whether you care about them or just about a performance.

You have prepared by knowing the space and where people will be seated. Can you see them? If you can, make eye contact briefly as you speak. Even when you first begin, find someone, make eye contact, and smile briefly. Let them know that you see them. If the room is large, such as a large sanctuary or an auditorium, some seats may be shaded or dark. You may be able to see everyone but not able to distinguish faces in a crowd. Look toward the places farthest away and smile. Look up at the balcony and let them know you see them. In the course of storytelling look up and gesture toward the people farthest away.

In concert halls and theaters around the world, the third balcony is where the most inexpensive seats are available. Often, these are the seats where students, or those unable to afford the best seats, are sitting. These are also the seats where those who have sacrificed everything to be there are seated. I like to call them the *seats of dreams.* When the lights are dimmed and the orchestra begins playing, the second and third balconies are the darkest. If you watch a great performer, you will notice that he or she often looks up, gestures, smiles, or sends a greeting to the "seats of dreams." It's a way of acknowledging those farthest away.

In the third balcony, a smile from the stage appears to every person as if the smile was just for her or him. An upward glance makes it seem that a performer is looking just at you. I know. I know because I was the person in the third balcony. I was the person scraping together every cent I had to be there—in the third balcony. I've never forgotten. I remember and look for those on the outside and hope that every one of them thinks I'm smiling just at him or her. I am.

Give Your Audience a Break

There are elements in every story that invite the audience to experience feelings in new ways. These are opportunities for the storyteller to invite listeners into the story and create memories. What are these elements? Where do they occur within the story?

We have looked at the importance of silence as a tool to emphasize or dramatize portions of the story. In the same manner, we have looked at pause and speed as clues to help the audience prepare for changes in the story. The ability to tell a story to a group of people and watch their reactions helps the storyteller regulate the use of silence, pause, and speed.

While regulating the flow and intensity of monologue will come naturally after a story is shared several times, how much to do so changes with each telling. Audience response dictates how long a silence should be. Lowering the volume and speed of the story are excellent tools to encourage closer listening, but the storyteller observes the audience to determine the length and depth of the change. The dynamics of each crowd may be different. The key is to tell the story using the most effective tools for each audience. A storyteller, like a teacher, does his or her best work when the learning patterns of the students or audience are the first consideration.

How do you know how your audience will respond? Most often you don't know until you are in front of them. However, as your storytelling experience broadens, you'll discover several distinct types of audiences. You will also learn to trust your instincts at the moment.

Recently, I had the opportunity to share stories with two very different audiences. The first was a gathering of Samoan, Tongan, and Native Hawaiian people. Before I was to speak, there were a few minutes of singing. The harmonies were rich and full and the singing full-throated and warm. I was greeted with warm applause. From the first words I spoke, the audience was responsive. Sad portions were marked by low murmurs. Humorous portions were marked by loud laughter and emotional events by tears. Before I had an opportunity to think much about "pulling the audience in," they were already there.

Sixteen hours later, I was standing in front of a crowd in the upper Midwest. The audience was made up of people from Danish and German extraction. Hard-working and serious, they had come from a business session into this time of storytelling. I was introduced with a sincere welcome. The audience was polite but noncommittal. Throughout our time together, there was some response, but nothing that would lead me to believe they were connecting with the stories. Rather than rely on the appearance of audience response, I relied on the integrity of the story, and concentrated on sharing both myself and the story with them. Over the period of the next day people sought me out recalling portions of the story that had been important to them. For several weeks afterward, cards and letters came from the audience who had listened quietly.

While audience response often dictates how we adjust the manner in which we tell a story, it is the story itself, and our commitment to it, that will determine effectiveness.

Moving Closer—Using Things and Touching People

Sometimes one simple thing has the visual strength to help connect spoken words and memory. In theater, the physical elements of a play are known as *props,* short for *property.* In storytelling, we use the same word to describe simple visual aids or storytelling tools. Most often storytelling props are single items, easily picked up and laid quietly aside.

One of the most important memories of my childhood involves my Dad's use of river rocks to teach me important elements of our culture. He would draw simple pictures on each stone and use them to tell me stories. I still have many of those stones, and I often pick them up, remembering those moments. Those memories are such an important element of my own development that I share that particular story when it might have meaning. It is a simple thing, really. As I speak, I put one hand in my pocket and lift out a stone, caressing it in my hand as I share the story. When I am done, I put it back into my pocket.

The use of the small stone has an interesting effect on me as well as on those listening to the story. For me, it is a gentle reminder of a wonderful person. I find myself holding the stone in much the same manner as my father did. While I am speaking, I subconsciously lift and hold the stone, and put it away at story's end with reluctance. It has a similar significance to the audience. From the time I remove the stone from my pocket, their eyes are drawn to the stone and to my face alternately. The stone enables the audience to step back many years and sit on my bed beside my father.

Props can enhance a story, as long as the audience can easily identify with them and they are not so numerous as to distract the audience from the story itself. Candles, small objects, a chair, a stool, a book, a piece of clothing, indeed any visual reminder of the story can have great meaning to those who are listening. Many times, audience members will ask rather shyly, "May I touch _____?" A small object becomes a way to touch an audience in a personal way, and make one more connection to you and the story.

It would seem that physical touch and storytelling would not go hand-in-hand. If the character of the storyteller is crucial to genuine storytelling, then physical touch is important to the event. Physical touch in the sense of touching hands is probably more realizable at the conclusion of the storytelling. Be present for as long as you are able. The physical access to a storyteller is important. If you have touched someone emotionally with a story, they will want some access to you, even for a brief moment.

Physical closeness has further connotations for the actual storytelling. Proximity to the audience is one way to create a feeling of closeness or distance. Use physical distance to convey emotional distance. As the story becomes more intimate, move closer to the audience, even if only a few feet. Lean close. The audience will gain a feeling of closeness even if you are on a stage. Creating intimacy is often creating the appearance of touch. The more you touch an audience, the more they will feel personally affected by the story—and the storyteller.

Old Stories Never Die: A Testimony

It sounds a bit absurd, but there is a reality in it. Old stories never die. As long as elements of the story are retold, the story lives, and in some ways so does the story-teller. It is not a quest for immortality or name recognition. It really is a statement of validity, genuineness, and credibility. The truth of the story guarantees that it is repeated.

The marvelous thing is that the story survives. Over the years, other storytellers may shape it or mold it to themselves, and the story may remain in one form, until another storyteller picks it up.

Truth survives. Truth as it relates to the human condition speaks to the human spirit. That is why I tell stories.

I treasure the compliments that people share with me. The ones that have the greatest value in my memory are not the "Oh, you're a wonderful storyteller" remarks. The ones that make me want to sit back in some sense of peace are those that say, "The story spoke to me. When the character did this. ..."

It means a great deal to me when someone recognizes that I often choose the vehicle of storytelling not because I don't have anything to say but because I have so much to say to the heart of another that it simply will not fit into an oratory or expository. I want to touch the heart of another person, and so I choose a way that enables me to say more than words. I choose a way that enables me to open up my heart so that another can see inside. The rightful access to a human spirit is first to open your own.

Storytelling calls me to credibility. At its best it is not a performance. It is an opening of self, at least a portion of self. I do not share stories that I do not seek to embody. I choose that accountability. As a storyteller, I celebrate the fact that I am not alone.

I begin every time with an audience with the same phrase. It is not a cute or pretty phrase but one that comes from the deepest part of my being. It comes through my people, through thousands of years, to each moment in time. It comes from understanding, *really understanding,* that the most important things in life are touching and giving away. So, each time as I stand before an audience, I make a commitment, even though most of them are never aware of what it means. I say, "I do not know if there is anything that you will carry away from my words, but I expect to be different because I have been with you. I have asked the Creator to show me things from your lives that will make me a better person. I am looking for those things, and I am certain that I will be a better man because I have been with you in this place." Always, *always,* there is something new that I have discovered before I go to sleep. I am not an entertainer. I am a storysharer.

Recently, in Alaska, several hundred miles from where I live, two Native men were among a group of walrus hunters providing meat for their village. The Bering Sea was rough, and the two men were separated in their boats from the other hunters. The outboard motor failed, and the high waves and winds carried the men farther out to sea.

The other hunters lost sight of the two men. After trying unsuccessfully to locate them, they returned to the village, with the storm increasing. The Coast Guard was notified, but the weather was too rough, and the men could not be located. The villagers gathered at the home of one of the elders and began to pray and "sing" for the men lost on the sea.

In the boat, the two men struggled to stay alive. The situation seemed hopeless. If they fell into the water, they would live for only a few minutes before they froze to death. In the back of one of their minds, a recollection began forming. It was a story. The words of the story heard from an elder many years ago began coming back to life. Part of the story included the construction of a sail. In the story, the hunter fashions a sail, shapes it to the proper form and attaches it to the boat. Sails were hardly used in their culture. It was an unusual story.

Quickly, the two men took black garbage bags and began forming them into the sail described in the story. They used a gaff pole to make a mast and each helped hold the "sail" as the story described. The boat began to turn. The wind caught the sail, and filled it full.

While the villagers were still praying and singing, and the Coast Guard waited for the weather to clear, two hunters walked through the entry of the elder's house. From a story, told long ago, they had fashioned a sail, the sail had caught the wind, and the wind had brought them home.

I am reminded that when I am lost, I pull from the reservoir of stories found deep in my memory. Many are from the Bible. Many are from my culture. Most are true. They are the experiences of others and myself, full of reality, laughter, joy, wisdom, sheer delight, and hidden truths.

I think that I have begun to wear my stories, as I have finally begun to wear my faith. They are part of my face, my choices, my actions, and my songs. I am not yet a storyteller, but I am on the journey to becoming one. If we chance on one another on this journey, let us celebrate all those who have gone before us. Let us delight in the truth shared in so many places in so many ways. Let us touch and give away. When you leave, take my stories if they have meaning to you. Polish them and carry them in your pockets like stones to give away to another traveler.

To paraphrase the Psalmist (Psalm 78):

> Listen to my stories.
> They are from experience and will help you as they
>   have helped me.
> They are not just words from my mouth.
> Listen.
> I am going to tell you a story.
> A Story of all stories, begun long ago.
> These are stories that we have heard while we were
>   being formed.

Our grandmother's grandmother, and grandfather's
grandfather told of these things.
It is time to share them with their children and chil-
dren's children.
We will tell to our children and those yet to be born,
"You are not alone.
Our God is strong and has done wonderful things."

Come, sit awhile and listen. Remember.
And when you remember, tell another,
So that they too will know the story,
And by remembering, tell someone else.

Part V

Word-Crafting—
A Storyteller's Box of Tools

The Internet

We live in an age of information, which also gives us access to stories, storytellers, and storytelling societies and organizations from around the world. The Internet provides an almost inexhaustible supply of information under "storytelling." Through the use of the World Wide Web, storytellers can share experiences, information, and stories with each other although separated by thousands of miles.

Storytelling organizations and societies are wonderful places to link with other storytellers. Storytelling festivals often provide one of the best ways to learn storytelling in a variety of settings. Digital storytelling can include sound/video files of storytellers as well as written versions of stories. Explore!

Internet addresses and information often change quickly. The following is a brief listing of categories and sites to make you aware of the variety of information available to you. As always, if addresses change, consult your Internet provider for an accurate listing of new or existing sites.

Digital Storytelling

http://www.storycenter.org/storyplace.html
(hosting digital storytelling, digital storytelling festivals, and storytellers)

http://www.dstory.com/dsf6/home.html
(features the Digital Storytelling Festival)

Storytelling Classes—Colleges and Universities

http://courses.unt.edu/efiga/STORYTELLING/WorldWideList.htm
(a thorough list of storytelling courses taught at colleges and universities around the world)

State and Regional Festivals/Organizations

http://www.bayareastorytelling.org/
(website of the [San Francisco] Bay Area Storytelling Festival)

http://www.connstorycenter.org/
(Connecticut Storytelling Center and Storytelling Festival site)

http://www.geocities.com/SoHo/Study/1578/index.html
(Dallas Storytelling Guild website)

http://www.srv.net/~telltale/guild.htm
(Storytelling Guild of Eastern Idaho)

http://www.storytelling.org/festival.html
(Illinois Storytelling Festival)

http://www.geocities.com/storiesinc/
(Storytelling Arts of Indiana)

http://www.downsks.net/storytelling.htm
(website of the Kansas Storytelling Festival)

http://www.lanes.org/
(League for the Advancement of New England Storytelling)

http://www.riverbendstorytelling.org/
(website of the Riverbend Storytelling Festival in West Bend, WI)

http://www.northlands.net/
(Upper-Midwest organization and storytelling conference)

http://www.storytellingcenter.com/
(International Storytelling Center; hosts the National Storytelling Festival in Jones-
borough, TN)

http://carbon.cudenver.edu/~jbowles/RMSF.html
(Rocky Mountain Storytelling Festival)

http://www.yukonstory.com/
(Yukon International Storytelling Festival)

Storytelling Technique and Information

http://darkwing.uoregon.edu/~leslieob/pizzaz.html
(University of Oregon site for poetry and storytelling ideas for teachers)

http://www.timsheppard.co.uk/story/
(an in-depth and rich site for storytellers of all levels)

http://www.story-telling.com/References/Resources.htm
(Internet storytelling resources and store)

http://www.web.net/~story/index.htm
(storytelling resources and original stories)

http://www.storynet.org/
(National Storytelling Network)

http://www.storytellingcenter.com/
(International Storytelling Center; hosts the National Storytelling Festival in Jones-
borough, TN)

Ethnic/Regional Storytelling

http://web.cocc.edu/cagatucci/classes/hum211/afrstory.htm
(African culture and storytelling)

http://www.home.aone.net.au/stories/
(Australian storytelling society; site includes aboriginal stories)

http://www.blueridgeonline.com/storylnk.htm
(wonderful site focusing on the Blue Ridge Mountains but also containing many stories and folklore from the region)

http://indigo.ie/~stories/index.htm
(Cape Clear Island International Storytelling Festival in Ireland)

http://www.hanksville.org/storytellers/traditional.html
(website including Native stories from many traditions)

http://www.cistory.org/
(California Indian Storytelling Association)

Storytelling for Youth

http://www.etsu.edu/stories/youtho.htm
(National Storytelling Youth Olympics)

http://www.storytellingarts.net/
(storytelling program for low-income children and youth and juvenile offenders)

Books

Long before the Internet, books provided one of the best means of sharing both stories and storytelling ideas. Storytelling books are seldom outdated, with information remaining valid over centuries. Libraries contain a wealth of resources for the fledgling storyteller as well as the professional. Below is a brief listing of resources. While none of them are complete in and of themselves (it would take too many pages!), each contains valuable information for learning and perfecting the various elements of storytelling.

The Art of the Story-Teller, by Marie L. Shedlock (Dover Publications, 1951). A storytelling classic. Rich ideas and insights from one of the premier storytellers of the twentieth century.

Just Enough to Make a Story, by Nancy Schimmel (Sisters' Choice Press, 1992). Strong suggestions for delivery.

Look What Happened to Frog: Storytelling in Education, by Pamela J. Cooper and Rives Collins (Gorsuch Scarisbrick, 1992). Highlights include suggestions for effective delivery and developing your own style.

Once Upon a Time: A Storytelling Handbook, by Lucille N. Breneman and Bren Breneman (Nelson-Hall Publishers, 1983). Highlights include suggestions for developing characterization, the use of visualization in storytelling, audience eye contact, and body language.

The Storytellers Start-Up Book, by Margaret Read MacDonald (August House, 1993).

Storytelling: A Guide for Teachers, by Catharine Farrell (Scholastic, 1991). A wonderful book for helping teachers in the incorporation of storytelling. Provides insight into visualizing characters. Currently out of print. Check with a library or other source for a copy of this book.

Storytelling Activities, by Norma J. Livo and Sandra A. Rietz (Libraries Unlimited, 1987). Strong ideas for learning movement as you tell stories. Currently out of print. Check with a library or other source for a copy of this book.

Storytelling: Process and Practice, by Norma J. Livo and Sandra A. Rietz (Libraries Unlimited, 1986). Good resource for developing strong practices or rituals in storytelling: physical space, flow, audience involvement, and so forth. Currently out of print. Check with a library or other source for a copy of this book.

Storytelling Step by Step, by Marsh Cassady (Resource Publications, 1990). Provides good insight into using personal experiences in storytelling and has an excellent chapter on delivery. This publisher has produced several works for storytelling in faith-based situations.

The Way of the Storyteller, by Ruth Sawyer (Viking Press, 1942). Good tools for delivery and moving past "technique."

Audiocassettes

Image-Nation, by Carol L Birch. Frostfire, 1992. A wonderful tool for understanding characters and situations in stories.

The storyteller's box of tools includes stories gathered from around the world, books, films, cassettes, DVDs, the Internet, and personal relationships with other storytellers. From the vast experiences of others, we add to our own experience, enriching both our stories and our lives.